BEYOND CONTAINMENT

BEYOND CONTAINMENT

Reconstructing European Security

Kim Edward Spiezio

LYNNE
RIENNER
PUBLISHERS

BOULDER
LONDON

To Janice and Nicholas,
my loves and my inspiration

Published in the United States of America in 1995 by
Lynne Rienner Publishers, Inc.
1800 30th Street, Boulder, Colorado 80301

and in the United Kingdom by
Lynne Rienner Publishers, Inc.
3 Henrietta Street, Covent Garden, London WC2E 8LU

Library of Congress Cataloging-in-Publication Data
Spiezio, K. Edward (Kim Edward), 1956–
Beyond containment : reconstructing European security / K. Edward Spiezio
p. cm.
Includes bibliographical references and index.
ISBN 1-55587-451-7 (alk. paper)
1. National security—Europe—International cooperation.
I. Title.
UA646.S648 1994
355'.03304—dc20 94-20271
CIP

British Cataloguing in Publication Data
A Cataloguing in Publication record for this book
is available from the British Library.

Printed and bound in the United States of America

∞ The paper used in this publication meets the requirements of the American National Standard for Permanence of Paper for Printed Library Materials Z39.48-1984.

CONTENTS

TABLES AND FIGURES

Tables

Figure

PREFACE

This book was written with two audiences in mind. First, I wanted to address students of U.S. foreign policy who are interested in better understanding the United States' response to the end of the Cold War in Europe. It is not unusual to hear contemporary observers characterize the recent course of U.S. foreign policy as essentially rudderless. In my view, however, this mistakes tactical maneuvering on the part of both the Bush and Clinton administrations for the absence of a coherent strategy. I seek to correct this misapprehension by outlining the fundamental features of the United States' post–Cold War strategy in Europe, which I label "the grand strategy of institutionalization."

Second, I also wanted to engage international relations theorists in a debate over the implications democracy holds for the prospects for international security cooperation. The end of the Cold War has prompted a number of scholars to call for the creation of a collective security system in Europe. Few studies, however, consider how democratization on the part of today's major powers may inhibit their ability to participate in this type of regime. This is an issue that should be of considerable interest to students of U.S. foreign policy as well since multilateral security institutions play a critical role within the context of U.S. post–Cold War strategy in Europe. By taking up this question, I hope to spark further research into how the domestic factors associated with democracy can both facilitate and complicate the multilateral management of international security problems.

I also hope to stimulate a dialogue between international relations theorists and foreign policy analysts by demonstrating how theory and empirical studies can be used to clarify the problems and possibilities associated with statecraft. A strategy, like any form of public policy, is fundamentally a type of theory that reflects decisionmakers' beliefs about the nature of cause-and-effect relationships in international politics. Hence, policy can and should be subjected to the same analytic criteria used in the evaluation of any theory. There is no guarantee, of course, that this type of rigorous analysis will lead to the selection of an appropriate strategy. Indeed, the sheer unpredictability of international and domestic politics renders the concept of good judgment highly suspect when it comes to the conduct of a nation's foreign policy. To forgo such an analysis, however, makes unclear how we might assess the relative merits of a strategy and risks placing ourselves at the mercy of the state and other so-called experts.

Several people have played an important role in helping me bring this project to a successful conclusion. First and foremost, I thank my wife, Janice, for being a source of encouragement and strength in my life. Without her unyielding moral support, I simply would have lacked the courage to persevere. Charles Taylor also deserves credit for lending me various types of institutional support during the year in which I wrote the manuscript. Charles went to great lengths to provide me with an opportunity to complete this research. For this, I thank him very much.

Substantively, this study is a reflection of the commitment to theory and practice long espoused by my mentor, colleague, and friend, Edward Weisband. Edward's scholarship has been a constant source of inspiration to me. I can only hope that this work begins to approach the high standards he has helped to establish in the field of U.S. foreign policy studies. I also must acknowledge the contribution Charles Walcott made in regard to the conclusion of this study. Quite useful comments were also received from Patrick Morgan and Charles Doran: Both read the entire manuscript and made valuable suggestions. The same can be said of my editor, Martha Peacock. Martha's gentle reassurances and ongoing encouragement were of considerable importance to me. In a similar vein, our departmental secretaries—Maxine, Terri, and Kim—deserve my unreserved thanks for helping to prepare various drafts of the manuscript.

Last, but certainly not least, I acknowledge the contribution the students of Virginia Tech have made to this study. This research is a direct outgrowth of my undergraduate teaching responsibilities in the areas of both U.S. foreign policy and international security. Virtually all of the material contained in this study has been presented at one time or another to the students of PSCI 3625 and 3734. Their questions and comments have played an invaluable role in helping me hone the analysis. For this service, I am in their debt.

Kim Spiezio

INTRODUCTION

U.S. foreign policy makers have responded to the end of the Cold War in Europe by reviving their long-standing goal of transforming the European states system into a liberal international society. It is a vision of Europe in which democracies, market-based economies, and international organizations combine to form a regional political order wherein the exercise of state power is restrained by an interlocking network of liberal norms and institutions located at the level of both domestic and international politics.

The attractiveness of this design lies in the possibilities it creates for enduring peace and prosperity in Europe. In essence, the emergence of a liberal international society would transform one of the most heavily militarized and conflict-prone regions of the world into a pluralistic security community overlaid by a single, integrated economy stretching from the Atlantic to the Urals. Obviously, such a development would serve the security and the economic interests of states located in both Europe and North America.

In pursuit of this goal, U.S. foreign policy makers have formulated a long-term, integrated strategy designed to facilitate the spread of liberal values and institutions in Europe. As yet unnamed by public officials, scholars, or the media, the approach perhaps can best be characterized as a grand strategy of institutionalization.[1] In practice, the strategy consists of two basic initiatives. First, the United States is endeavoring to promote and consolidate the democratization and marketization of state-society relations in countries located throughout the eastern half of the European continent. Second, U.S. policymakers also are supporting efforts to broaden and deepen the role international institutions play in the management of regional security, economic, and social issues. In combination, these initiatives represent an ambitious attempt to establish an overarching normative and institutional framework on the Continent that will serve, over time, to liberalize the constitutive principles of political association both within and among the states of Europe.

1

The Purpose of the Study

One purpose of this study is to document the emergence of the grand strategy of institutionalization in 1989–1990 and its subsequent embrace by the Clinton administration. This is done primarily through an analysis of public statements and policy pronouncements made by senior members of both the Bush and Clinton administrations. This portion of the study examines the strategic beliefs underlying the United States' response to the end of the Cold War and indicates how these beliefs combine to form a grand strategy that ultimately will transform the European states system into a liberal international society.

Another purpose of the study is to examine some of the practical steps U.S. foreign policy makers have taken to implement the strategy. Here, particular attention is paid to the United States' efforts to develop a new security architecture in Europe by broadening and deepening the role international institutions play in the management of regional security affairs. This focus is warranted because multilateral security institutions (e.g., the North Atlantic Treaty Organization [NATO], the United Nations [UN], and the Conference on Security and Cooperation in Europe [CSCE]) are assigned a key role within the context of the grand strategy of institutionalization; to wit, these organizations are charged with the responsibility for managing the domestic and international conflicts that may arise during the process of liberalization in Eastern Europe and the former Soviet Union.

The study also raises a series of questions about the viability of multilateral security institutions in the post–Cold War era. Conceptually, Europe's emerging security architecture constitutes a nascent collective security system.[2] While in principle this type of regime is well suited to carry out the order-keeping tasks envisioned by U.S. foreign policy makers, in practice multilateral institutions are characterized by a number of well-known obstacles to cooperation that can limit their effectiveness as a tool for the management of international security issues.

Many analysts dismiss such concerns, however, by arguing that contemporary systemic and domestic conditions in Europe should enable states to overcome the cooperation problems that have undermined collective security systems in the past. Of the factors cited in support of this claim, none is more important than the fact that all of the major powers of Europe currently are led by democratically oriented governments. This is an unprecedented political development that presumably has established a domestic political foundation conducive to the multilateral management of European security affairs.

I challenge this conclusion by arguing that under certain systemic circumstances domestic political factors can inhibit a democratic government's ability to participate in a collective security system. I support this claim by presenting insights derived from the international relations literature that suggest that contemporary systemic and domestic conditions may render a collective security system an unviable political option from the standpoint of liberal states and societies. Hence, I conclude that the multilateral institutions comprising Europe's nascent collective security system are likely to be plagued by repeated acts of buck-passing on the part of the major powers. I also contend that this problem will be, in part, a consequence of the fact that these states are led by democratically oriented governments. The study concludes with a brief discussion of the implications the argument holds for the grand strategy of institutionalization and the future of the European states system.

Europe and the United States: The Enduring Link

Ultimately, this study seeks to make a contribution to both our understanding of contemporary U.S. foreign policy and the literature on international cooperation. The end of the Cold War has been greeted with a flood of books and articles concerning the future of U.S. foreign policy. Most of these analyses, however, have been largely normative in character. That is, the authors prescribe various steps policymakers should take in the name of promoting U.S. interests. There is nothing wrong with this tack, but it does divert attention from the actual policies that the United States has been pursuing in regard to Europe.

This is a serious oversight because, historically, the United States' role in international politics has been defined primarily in relation to the European states system (Craig, 1977; Rostow, 1993). For example, after gaining independence, Americans defined themselves largely in opposition to Europe. The U.S. experiment was represented as a conscious attempt to break with European practices at the level of both domestic and international politics (Schlesinger, 1986: 3–22). Conceptually, "Americanism" was framed as a revolutionary alternative to the autocratic and militaristic practices long associated with the European states system (Paine, 1775/1938). This understanding of the United States' broader purpose in the international system, in turn, helped to spawn the distinctive strategy of isolationism (Crabb, 1986: 1–14).

Isolationism, of course, sought to insulate first the United States itself, and subsequently the entire Western Hemisphere, from the day-to-day machinations associated with Europe's classical balance-of-power system. In doing so, the strategy was designed to provide breathing space for the growth and development of the United States (Washington, 1796/1940: 214–238). At the same time, however, isolationism would facilitate the promotion of new principles of international association that literally could revolutionize the nature of international relations in the realm of both economics and security (see Monroe, 1823/1896: 207–220).

This phase in U.S. foreign policy reached its climax at the end of World War I. Under the leadership of Woodrow Wilson, the United States made its first concerted attempt to transform the nature of the European states system (Osgood, 1953). At the Versailles peace conference, Wilson endeavored to lay the foundation for a liberal international society in Europe by establishing a collective security system that would replace the balance of power as the main instrumentality of regional security (Levin, 1968). Ultimately, however, this revolutionary undertaking was defeated by a combination of domestic and international obstacles (Ambrosius, 1987), whereupon the United States reverted to its historic role as a regional power whose security-related activities were confined largely to the Western Hemisphere.

Following the end of World War II, the United States' stance toward the European states system underwent a fundamental transformation as U.S. foreign policy makers opted to become deeply involved in the management of European security issues (DePorte, 1986). Responding to the challenge posed by the Soviet Union, the United States became an active participant in the European states system; and for the next five decades, the United States' role in international politics would be defined largely in opposition to the Soviet Union. During this period, of course, the grand strategy of containment stood as the conceptual centerpiece of U.S. statecraft (Gaddis, 1982).

In 1989, this phase in U.S. foreign policy came to an abrupt and unexpected end. Over the last four years, a series of revolutionary geopolitical developments have fundamentally transformed the European states system. The dissolution of the Soviet Union has unleashed forces that have destabilized political, economic, and military arrangements throughout the Continent. Hence, for the third time this century, the United States is confronted with the task of redefining its role in Europe.

As this brief review suggests, the fate of Europe and the United States are bound by a transatlantic link that remains as strong today as it was in the eighteenth century. This enduring relationship is a consequence of a simple, yet fundamental, geopolitical fact: Historically, most of the world's major military powers have been located in Europe. For all intents and purposes, recent changes have not diminished the validity of this proposition (Waltz, 1993). Hence, the stability of this region of the world still holds enormous consequences for the United States and its people.

Given the importance of this transatlantic relationship, the United States' response to the end of the Cold War in Europe deserves careful study. A state's selection of a grand strategy holds enormous consequences for its own citizens as well as for other members of the international community. By embracing a particular approach, a government commits itself to an enduring course of action that inevitably affects the nature of state-society relations in its own country and perhaps even the character of the state itself. At the same time, of course, a state's grand strategy will have significant implications for the way it relates to, and interacts with, other countries.

These are familiar themes in the literature on U.S. foreign policy. In the nineteenth century, for example, the strategy of isolationism was justified, in part, by concerns about how active participation in Europe's balance-of-power system might adversely affect the evolution of the state and its relationship with U.S. society (Crabb, 1986: 3).[3] Similar concerns have been voiced in the post–World War II era by critics of the grand strategy of containment. Seen from this perspective, the pursuit of containment has led to, inter alia, the growth of a "national security state" as well as to precipitous national economic decline (Yergin, 1977; Kennedy, 1987: 347–437). The international consequences of the United States' security strategies are, of course, the subject of a voluminous literature. Isolationism and containment both have been praised by some, and pilloried by others, for the impact they have had on the historical evolution of international politics. These considerations simply reinforce the importance of understanding the problems and possibilities implicit in the United States' grand strategy of institutionalization.

Democracies Don't Fight, but Can They Cooperate?

This study also seeks to make a contribution to the literature on international cooperation. Many theorists presume that democracies are ideally suited to cooperate in the realm of security (e.g., Flynn and Scheffer, 1990). Democracies, for example, rarely fight one another (Doyle, 1983) and their political systems are relatively transparent (Cowhey, 1993). Hence, democratization should serve to ameliorate many of the concerns and fears that have tended to inhibit international security cooperation in the past. Moreover, political homogeneity should be conducive to the emergence of a normative consensus on the part of states about the "essential features of a desirable international order" (Kupchan and Kupchan, 1991: 146). In theory, this shared sense of purpose should serve to encourage and sustain security cooperation on the part of democracies as well.

In light of this, democratization on the part of the major powers would seem to establish a domestic political foundation conducive to the collaborative acts that are essential to the success of multilateral security institutions. This conclusion, however, generally ignores the obstacles domestic factors can pose to international cooperation. This, of course, is a blind spot that has characterized the study of international cooperation for years (Milner, 1992: 488–495; Evans, Jacobson, and Putnam, 1993). It is a potentially serious omission when assessing the prospects for security co-operation on the part of democracies.

Democratization generally enhances the role domestic factors play in the formulation and implementation of public policy (Katzenstein, 1977; Krasner, 1978). Recent research indicates that this proposition holds in the realm of security policy as well as in other issue-areas (e.g., Evangelista, 1989; Barnett, 1990; Risse-Kappen, 1991, 1993; Snyder, 1991; Katzenstein and Okawara, 1993). To pursue a given security strategy, democratic governments need to mobilize and maintain public support. This dimension of statecraft is crucial within the context of a democratic political system because liberal norms place the state in a subordinate position vis-à-vis society (Mastanduno, Lake, and Ikenberry, 1989; Barnett, 1990). Hence, it is incumbent upon foreign policy makers to establish a clear linkage between their security-related activities and some broader social purpose. Put differently, democratic governments must legitimize their policy choices by explaining how and why these initiatives serve the "national interest" (George, 1989). In the absence of this, it will be difficult for the state to justify its extractive demands (e.g., men, money, and material) to groups and individuals located in society.

This is an important point within the context of the post–Cold War era because a collective security system depends heavily upon a minilateralist core of major-power cooperation. It is the major powers, after all, who provide the bulk of the military capabilities that provide the institution with its credibility as a deterrent to aggression. Hence, unless the major powers are willing and able to collaborate in the realm of security, this type of regime is likely to prove ineffective as a tool for the management of international security problems (Morgan, 1993: 352).

This highlights a dilemma that holds potentially important implications for multilateral security institutions in the post–Cold War era. The major powers of contemporary Europe are more secure from external attack than states have ever been in the history of the interstate system. This unprecedented level of security stems principally from three factors: the advent of nuclear weapons, the declining economic utility of territorial expansion, and the spread of democracy among the major powers. Notice that these factors serve to diminish the likelihood of major-power conflict in Europe regardless of whether or not a collective security system is established. Hence, the security of the major powers is not contingent upon the existence of the regime; their political independence and territorial integrity are underwritten by a combination of technological and political developments that stand independent of any institutional arrangement. As a consequence, the existence of a collective security system is unlikely to enhance the security of the major powers to any significant degree.

The political salience of this claim is compounded by the fact that democratic governments need to generate and sustain domestic support if they are to actively participate in a collective security system. Yet, how can the state convince members of its society to bear a disproportionate share of the costs of an institution that is unlikely to significantly enhance the security of their own country? Unfortunately, cooperation theorists and security analysts generally have failed to address this problem and the implications it holds for the likelihood of enduring security cooperation on the part of the democratic major powers comprising post–Cold War Europe.

The present study tackles this question by developing a theoretical argument that links domestic political support for collective security institutions to the polarity of the international political system and the nature of military technology. In essence, the argument suggests that the prospects for democratic cooperation vary along with the nature of the international security environment confronting states. To wit, under conditions of multipolarity and defense dominance, it will become extremely difficult for democratic governments to establish and maintain a viable system of collective security. Hence, unlike studies that link the future of multilateral security institutions to the relative decline of U.S. power or other factors located exclusively at the systemic level of analysis (e.g., Calleo, 1987), the present study maintains that the fate of Europe's nascent collective security system is more likely to be determined by the domestic political factors that currently characterize the major powers. Democracies may never fight, but this does not mean that they always will manifest domestic political support for participating in the multilateral management of international security problems.

The United States and Collective Security

This argument also has implications for the future of U.S. security policy in the post–Cold War era. Recently, Robert Jervis (1991/92: 41) has suggested that in order "to predict the future of world politics . . . [we must first] predict the future of American foreign policy." If this is the case, the task would appear to be hopeless. Few subjects have attracted as much scholarly attention, yet remained so impervious to the development of theory, as has U.S. foreign policy. The enormous literature on this subject is characterized by a heterogeneous assortment of conceptual frameworks, ad hoc hypotheses, and discrete empirical findings suggesting a wide range of variables and causal processes that might be useful for explaining U.S. foreign policy outcomes (see Ikenberry, 1989; Kegley and Wittkopf, 1991). Unfortunately, these islands of theory have yet to be linked in any theoretically meaningful or coherent way. As it stands, there is virtually no consensus as to how we might explain, let alone predict, the course of U.S. foreign policy (Gaddis, 1990).

The present study does not pretend to offer a grand theory of U.S. foreign policy. Indeed, it is probably impossible to formulate such a theory. A more realistic, and potentially profitable approach is "to search for models or theories that operate, hold, or are valid only under certain explicitly prescribed conditions" (Most and Starr, 1989: 99). The argument linking domestic structures and collective security provides such an opportunity. In principle, it can account for variations in the United States' stance toward collective security institutions by pointing to specific systemic factors and the effect these factors exert on the United States' domestic political processes. On the basis of this model, some probabilistic statements can also be made about the stance U.S. foreign policymakers are likely to take when it comes to the task of international conflict management in post–Cold War Europe.

In essence the theory predicts that, under existing systemic conditions, the United States is likely to adopt an isolationist approach when it comes to the security of countries located in Eastern Europe and the former Soviet Union. This is not to suggest that the United States will seek to withdraw completely from world affairs; nor does it mean that U.S. foreign policy makers will refuse to play any managerial role internationally. Isolationism was not characterized by these attributes in the 1920s and 1930s, and there is no reason to believe that it would be in the future either.

An isolationist approach, however, will impose some important limitations upon the security-related role the United States assumes in regard to post–Cold War Europe. Historically, isolationism has been characterized by an unwillingness on the part of the United States to extend binding security commitments to other countries and a general reluctance to engage in military interventions outside of the Western Hemisphere (Tucker, 1972). The argument advanced in the present study suggests that this is the stance that the United States is most likely to take in regard to Eastern Europe and the former Soviet Union. Moreover, the study also presents anecdotal evidence that suggests the Clinton administration already has begun to manifest such isolationist tendencies when it comes to the task of international security management in the eastern half of the Continent.

The Plan of the Study

I begin with a discussion of the grand strategy of institutionalization. Chapter 1 lays out the internal architecture of the strategy and advances a tentative explanation for both the timing and the content of this approach.

The discussion also highlights the prominent role multilateral security institutions are supposed to play within the context of this ambitious attempt to transform Europe into a liberal international society.

Chapter 2 chronicles the steps U.S. policymakers have taken to build a new security architecture in post–Cold War Europe. This portion of the analysis examines the United States' efforts to: (1) establish a new arms control regime in Europe, (2) develop a strategic partnership with the Russian Federation, and (3) broaden and deepen the role international institutions play in the management of regional security affairs.

Chapter 3 provides a theoretical discussion of the strengths and weaknesses associated with Europe's nascent collective security system. As part of the analysis, I also examine arguments that purport to explain why democratization on the part of the major powers constitutes a domestic political foundation favorable to the formation of a collective security system in post–Cold War Europe.

Chapter 4 presents a theoretical argument that links domestic political support for collective security institutions to a set of factors located at the level of the international system. The argument incorporates insights derived from the growing literature on state-society relations and the implications these factors have when it comes to the foreign policy behavior of democratic states. The model is then applied to contemporary international circumstances to indicate why prevailing systemic and domestic conditions are not conducive to the far-reaching acts of security cooperation that are called for within the context of multilateralism. It also explains why these factors are likely to exert their greatest effects in the case of the United States.

Chapter 5 operationalizes the concept of isolationism and presents evidence that indicates the Clinton administration has begun to exhibit isolationist tendencies when it comes to the management of security problems in Eastern Europe and the former Soviet Union. We also consider the implications this stance may have for the United States' ability to exert leadership in post–Cold War Europe. The chapter concludes with a discussion of the consequences this dilemma may hold for the future of both the European states system and the United States' grand strategy of institutionalization.

Before proceeding, I would like to point out that this study does not formally test any particular theory of international politics or foreign policy; nor was it intended to advance some new theoretical approach to the study of U.S. statecraft. Instead, the analysis uses existing theories as heuristic devices for assessing the problems and possibilities associated with the grand strategy of institutionalization. This tack may disappoint some readers given the importance scholars attach to the development and refinement of theory. While I share in this commitment to the pursuit of explanatory knowledge, the type of evaluative research presented here is nonetheless valuable (Vasquez, 1986).

As we take stock of the field of security studies, it quickly becomes clear that one of its greatest strengths lies in its ability to expose erroneous beliefs about the nature of cause-and-effect relationships in international politics. Over the years, researchers have done a masterful job of debunking a large number of intuitively plausible hypotheses concerning the causes of war and peace. The importance of this contribution should not be underestimated. By analyzing the abductive assumptions, logical consistency, and empirical content of numerous theories, scholars have managed to reveal that much of what passes for knowledge is little more than unsubstantiated beliefs and/or politically motivated myths propagated by self-interested actors (Posen, 1984; Snyder, 1991).

Over time, these revelations have tended to promote a more sophisticated perspective on the part of both scholars and statespeople in regard to the subject of national and international security. As a consequence, we all have become more discriminating when it comes to evaluating the relative merits of the various strategic beliefs we encounter in the marketplace of ideas. Hence, by underscoring the limits of our knowledge about the dynamics and processes associated with international politics, scholars play an invaluable role in informing public debates over the wisdom of various national security policies. This broader social purpose stands at the heart of the present study.

Notes

1. In a speech at Johns Hopkins University, National Security Adviser Anthony Lake characterized this approach as a "strategy of enlargement." The label, however, did not capture the imagination of the media. Hence, the term rarely is used in public debates concerning the Clinton administration's strategy in Europe. I prefer the term "institutionalization" because it more accurately reflects the United States' long-term goal in Europe. Analysts typically characterize grand strategies on the basis of their intended political effects (e.g., containment). In the present case, U.S. foreign policy makers hope to create a liberal international society in Europe by promoting liberal political and economic institutions at the level of both domestic and international politics.

2. This conceptualization is based upon Kupchan and Kupchan's (1991: 119) contention that any organization that "operates on the notion of all against one and relies on the collective action to resist aggression" can be categorized as a collective security institution. As indicated in Chapter 3, NATO, CSCE, and the UN all are premised upon these principles. For a criticism of this approach as vitiating the concept of collective security, see Zelikow (1992: 27–28) and Betts (1992: 15–16). The term "nascent collective security system" is borrowed from Robert Jervis's discussion of major-power concerts. In Jervis's usage (1985: 78), the concept

refers to an international arrangement that creates "some expectation of support from third parties" whenever a state's security is jeopardized.

3. Prior to World War II, the conventional wisdom held that isolationism was essential to both the United States' viability as a democracy and the country's economic welfare. This conviction was rooted in the belief that isolationism diminished the prospects for

> foreign intervention in the political and economic affairs of the nation; the growth of militarism and escalating armaments expenditures; the loss of freedoms guaranteed by the Bill of Rights and other liberties; the emergence of presidential dictatorship and the consequent decline of Congress; a steadily mounting national debt; internal divisiveness and acute political factionalism; [and] economic retrogression. (Crabb, 1986: 3)

1

THE GRAND STRATEGY
OF INSTITUTIONALIZATION

The United States' strategy toward post–Cold War Europe is premised upon three fundamental beliefs. First, democratization on a continental-wide scale will serve to pacify and stabilize the European states system at the level of both domestic and international politics. Second, democratization entails a long-term process of evolutionary change that must be bolstered by corresponding economic reforms and an ongoing attempt to strengthen regional security. Third, these mutually reinforcing initiatives can best be supported by broadening and deepening the role international institutions play in the management of European political, economic, and security affairs.

This chapter examines the key components of the grand strategy of institutionalization as articulated by members of both the Bush and Clinton administrations. The purposes of this discussion are: to document the emergence of the strategy in 1989–1990 and its subsequent embrace by the Clinton administration; to outline the generative logic that weaves the internal architecture of the strategy together; and to provide a preliminary explanation for both the timing and the content of the strategy. I begin, however, with a brief discussion of grand strategy as an analytic concept.

The Concept of Grand Strategy

A grand strategy can best be defined as an enduring program of action designed to enhance state security through the coordinated use of diplomatic, economic, and military instruments.[1] In the words of Paul Kennedy (1991: 5), "the crux of grand strategy lies therefore in policy, that is, in the capacity of the nation's leaders to bring together all of the elements, both military and non-military, for the preservation and enhancement of the nation's long-term . . . interests."

Analytically, a grand strategy can be characterized in terms of an internal architecture wherein discrete diplomatic, economic, and military policies stand as interrelated components of a single, overarching design (see George, 1989: 586–587). On the basis of this conceptualization, analysts are able to specify the functional role each policy is to play in support of the state's strategic objectives and to indicate how the individual policy instruments are designed to relate to, and interact with, one another in pursuit of these goals.

More important, by specifying the internal architecture of a grand strategy, analysts also can gain insights into the beliefs decisionmakers hold about the nature of cause-and-effect relationships in the realm of security. A grand strategy, like any form of public policy, can be treated as if it were a type of theory: a means-ends chain that reflects the assumptions and beliefs held by policymakers (Posen, 1984: 13; George, 1993). Seen from this perspective, a grand strategy can be represented as more than simply a complex of policies; it also can be regarded as an interrelated set of propositions that "identifies the objectives that must be achieved to produce security and describes the political and military actions that are believed to lead to this goal" (Walt, 1989: 6).[2] Hence, to study the subject of grand strategy is to inquire into both the theory and the practice of a state's national security policy.

Admittedly, there are some important methodological challenges associated with this task. Like all concepts, grand strategy is fundamentally a heuristic device analysts employ to impose a sense of order and coherence in regard to discrete phenomena that might otherwise seem to be unrelated. Hence, when scholars use the concept, there is always some risk that they will impute an underlying design, or logic, to a congeries of policies that the decisionmakers themselves were either unaware of or never intended.[3] This, of course, raises the possibility that analysts may reach spurious conclusions about either the existence of a grand strategy or its substantive content.

This problem is exacerbated by the fact that governments rarely produce a single document, or strategic blueprint, that clearly and unambiguously outlines their overall national security strategy. As a result, scholars engaged in this type of research must rely principally upon "the process of deduction while sifting through the papers of those who actually participated in the process by which grand strategy was made and carried out" (Hattendorf, 1991: 12–13). Put differently, archival research traditionally has been an indispensable tool for the student of grand strategy.

The evidence presented in this chapter has been derived largely from primary documents released by the United States government.[4] For the student of contemporary U.S. foreign policy, there is little choice but to rely on such sources. In the present case, for example, very few of the internal documents (e.g., memorandums, reports, meeting transcripts) that would be useful for an understanding of U.S. strategy in Europe have been declassified and released to the public. Moreover, none of the key members of the Bush administration have yet to publish their memoirs.[5] Hence, to undertake this type of study, there are few practical alternatives but to rely on information released by the government itself.[6]

Obviously, a study based on this type of documentary evidence must confront the issues of reliability and validity. Public officials, of course, have been known to use these media for a variety of purposes, including deception. This is an especially important concern in the present case since I rely heavily upon these sources to infer decisionmakers' beliefs about the means and ends of the United States' post–Cold War strategy in Europe. Hence, it is important to be clear about the methodological procedures to which I adhered in analyzing these documents.

There are two basic ways of addressing the issues of reliability and validity raised by this type of study. First, we can assess the logical consistency of the public statements and policy pronouncements made by senior-level policymakers (e.g., presidents, national security advisers, secretaries of state). Analytically, the plausibility of our conclusions concerning the existence and/or content of a grand strategy will increase if we find an ongoing pattern of convergent elite policy statements concerning: (1) the nature of a state's security objectives, and (2) the combination of policy instruments needed to achieve these goals (Kegley, 1987: 258–260). Since a grand strategy constitutes an enduring program of action, this type of analysis must be done across members of the same administration as well as across one administration to the next.

Second, we can examine the logical consistency that exists between the public statements made by senior-level policymakers and the state's actual foreign policy behavior. This also should be done both within and across administrations. The "congruence procedure" (George, 1979: 105) provides an indication of the extent to which state practice corresponds to official policy pronouncements. Here again, the reliability and validity of our conclusions in regard to either the existence or the content of a grand strategy will be strengthened if we find an ongoing pattern of foreign policy activities that is consistent with convergent elite policy statements concerning the means and ends of the state's national security program.[7]

Both of these procedures have been utilized in the present study. I have examined nearly 500 documents pertaining to U.S. policy in Europe that have been released by the United States government since January 1989. These include speeches, the text of treaties and other international agreements signed by the United States, press releases, and press conference transcripts. Each document was analyzed separately and then cross-referenced in an attempt to assess the degree of elite consensus in regard to the means and ends of the United States' policy toward post–Cold War Europe. Next, the textual analysis was supplemented by a review of the diplomatic record as reported in the *Washington Post* and the *New York Times*. The goal here was to determine the extent to which the actual conduct of U.S. foreign policy has been consistent with the ideas expressed by senior-level policymakers.

The remainder of the chapter is devoted to a discussion of the results of this analysis. The evidence indicates that, since the end of 1989, U.S. foreign policy makers have been remarkably consistent when it comes to their public representations of the United States' strategy toward post–Cold War Europe. The following sections outline the key components of the grand strategy of institutionalization as articulated publicly by members of both the Bush and Clinton administrations.

The Internal Architecture

The first public presentation of the basic conceptual framework that would guide the United States' response to the end of the Cold War in Europe was provided in a series of speeches delivered by then Secretary of State James Baker in the months following the fall of the Berlin Wall.[8] Of these, Baker's addresses before the Berlin Press Club (December 12, 1989) and the World Affairs Council (March 30, 1990) stand as the most comprehensive and coherent presentations of the strategy the United States would employ to "consolidate the fruits of this peaceful revolution and provide the architecture for continued peaceful change."[9]

The seminal quality of these addresses is indicated by the nature of subsequent policy statements made by members of both the Bush and Clinton administrations. Despite occasional tactical differences over the implementation of the strategy, no senior-level policymaker has yet to challenge the overarching strategic design elaborated in these speeches. In light of the subsequent significance of these speeches, the discussion begins with a detailed analysis of the ideas contained in them.[10]

"Beyond containment lies democracy" (*AFP*, 1990: 12). With these words, James Baker signaled the beginning of a fundamental change in the nature of the United States' strategic goals in Europe. To wit, the grand strategy of containment was being abandoned in favor of a "new mission: . . . the promotion and consolidation of democracy" (*AFP*, 1990: 12).[11] Instead of orienting U.S. foreign policy around the task of containing the expansion of Soviet power and influence, the United States would now devote its resources to the achievement of a new objective: the construction of a "democratic international society" in Europe (*AFP*, 1990: 17). In essence, the United States' long-range goal was to create a regional political order wherein "free men and free governments" would stand as the basic "building blocks" of the European states system (*AFP*, 1989: 300).

In these speeches, Baker (*AFP,* 1989: 300; *AFP,* 1990: 12–13) characterized democratization as the key to the future of post–Cold War Europe. The spread of liberal values and institutions would have a stabilizing and pacifying effect at the level of both domestic and international politics. Internally, democratic institutions would serve to legitimize the exercise of state authority in societies undergoing revolutionary changes. Similarly, liberal norms would diminish the likelihood of domestic political violence by guaranteeing the rights of all citizens, including minorities. Democratization, of course, also would serve to limit the potential for international conflict by constraining the state's ability to use force as a foreign policy instrument. These convictions were articulated most clearly in Baker's comments to the World Affairs Council in Dallas.

> Democracy's reliance upon the individual is reciprocated by the individual's consent to the rule of democratic government. That government is, therefore, considered legitimate in the most basic political sense—both lawful and proper. . . . A democratic society also is characterized by the rule of law and by tolerance of diversity, a tolerance that protects individual rights from abuse, whether from an arbitrary minority or a tyrannical majority . . . There [also] is a self-renewal, a self-corrective element in the democratic process which allows us to overcome blunders and correct the course. . . . [Hence] it can operate not only to ensure domestic progress but also to encourage international harmony. Free people cherishing democratic values are unlikely to go to war with one another. (*AFP,* 1990: 13)[12]

While democratization was framed as central to the future of the European states system, Baker also contended that political reforms and free elections would not be enough to ensure the success of this undertaking in the eastern half of the Continent; the process of democratization had to be supported by corresponding efforts to promote economic reforms and to strengthen regional security. To underscore this point, Baker invoked the metaphor of "political geometry."

> Geometry teaches us that the triangle is the most solid configuration. The political geometry of successful democracy should teach us that a free society must be upheld by economic progress and basic security. War and poverty are the great opponents of democratic rules, democratic tolerance, and individual rights. . . . We must therefore build up the economic and security aspects of the new democracies even as the political base is put into place. . . . Only a strategy that buttresses democracy with economic reforms and greater international security can give us the strength for the tough transitions that will transform the revolutions of 1989 into the democracies of the 1990s. (*AFP,* 1990: 12)

As part of this discussion, Baker also revealed his conviction that these mutually reinforcing initiatives could best be achieved by broadening and deepening the role international institutions play in the management of regional political, economic, and security affairs. During his address to the Berlin Press Club, Baker outlined the distinctive contribution that NATO, CSCE, and the European Community could make to the process of transforming Europe into a democratic international society.[13]

NATO's principal mission, for example, would be to help create a regional security environment free of intimidation and the threat of invasion (*AFP*, 1989: 301). This was to be done by enhancing NATO's role as a forum wherein "nations cooperate to negotiate, implement, verify, and extend agreements between East and West" (*AFP*, 1989: 301). Baker expressed a particular interest in establishing "consultative arrangements" whereby the members of NATO and other states could engage in a continuing dialogue concerning the management of regional conflicts and the pursuit of arms control initiatives in Europe (*AFP*, 1989: 301).

CSCE, on the other hand, was to take the lead in promoting human rights and free elections in the eastern half of the Continent (*AFP*, 1989: 304). In Baker's view, the institution's overarching mission would be "to make democracy the legitimizing principle for all of Europe" (*AFP*, 1990: 16). At the same time, however, Baker also envisioned CSCE playing an important role in the realm of security. Through its sponsorship of conferences relating to confidence-building measures in Europe, for example, CSCE could promote greater transparency among member states that, in turn, would bolster the prospects for international cooperation in the realm of security and in other areas (*AFP*, 1989: 303).

Finally, the European Community would be in the forefront of efforts to promote both the marketization and the democratization of Eastern European countries. In Baker's view, the Community's role as a catalyst for change was critical. In essence, political and economic reforms were to be propelled by rewarding those states that "take steps toward democracy and economic liberty" with some form of associative status vis-à-vis the European Community (*AFP*, 1989: 302).

Conceptually, the ideas contained in these speeches can be characterized in terms of a generative logic whereby a liberal international society emerges as a consequence of coordinated efforts to: (1) promote the democratization and marketization of state-society relations in countries located throughout the eastern half of the Continent, and (2) broaden and deepen the role international institutions play in the management of military, political, economic, and social issues in the region. Taken together, the initiatives represent an ambitious attempt to liberalize the constitutive principles of political association both within and between the states of Europe. In essence, the Bush administration's strategy toward post–Cold War Europe was oriented to the goal of establishing a regional political order wherein the exercise of state power would be restrained by an interlocking network of liberal norms and institutions located at the level of both domestic and international politics.

The attractiveness of this design lies in the possibilities it creates for peace and prosperity in Europe. History indicates that democracies rarely go to war with one another (Russett, 1993). Hence, there are compelling reasons to believe that democratization on a continental-wide scale would serve to pacify the European states system. Moreover, by incorporating Eastern European states firmly into the liberal international economic order, the strategy also promises to unleash productive forces and opportunities for international exchange that could serve to reproduce the steady but moderate economic growth that stood at the core of regional stability throughout most of the post–World War II era.

The strategic significance of these potential developments, from the standpoint of the United States' security and economic interests, should not be underestimated. Historically, war and revolution in Europe have posed the single greatest threat to the security and welfare of the United States. The twentieth century speaks eloquently to this point. For the past eighty years, the stability of the European states system has been jeopardized by the imperialistic practices of autocratic states bent on increasing the scope of their power and influence on the Continent. The United States has felt the consequences of this ongoing struggle just as assuredly as have the states located in the region. The most conspicuous U.S. sacrifices, of course, can be found in the blood and money the United States has spent in defense of European stability. The emergence of a liberal international society in Europe would lighten the demands placed upon the United States (and other states) considerably by creating an environment in which the rule of law prevails over the law of the jungle. Under such circumstances, the potential for war and revolution in Europe should decline precipitously.

Given the data limitations mentioned at the beginning of this chapter, we presently are unable to document the decisionmaking process associated with the emergence of the grand strategy of institutionalization at the end of 1989. In order to provide a satisfactory account of both the timing and the content of the strategy, we would need access to internal documents that simply are unavailable. While strategy can be regarded as essentially a cognitive phenomenon, it is formulated within the context of political, economic, and social factors that inevitably affect the decisionmaking process (see Kennedy, 1991). Hence, strategizing is by no means a purely intellectual exercise; it is the product of an inherently political process that can be understood only by examining the relevant archival materials.

On the basis of the available evidence, however, it is possible to advance a tentative explanation for both the timing and the content of the grand strategy of institutionalization. The former can be attributed to the fall of the Berlin Wall, which the Bush administration appears to have interpreted as a sign of the Soviet Union's irrevocable commitment to fundamentally change the status quo in Europe. The content of the strategy may be a consequence of the lessons that U.S. foreign policy makers have derived from the post–World War II era. The following sections elaborate on both of these possibilities.

The Timing of the Strategy

As the Bush administration took office in January 1989, an air of uncertainty surrounded the future of U.S.–Soviet relations. During Ronald Reagan's last years as president, there clearly had been an improvement in the overall tone of the superpower relationship (Cannon, 1991: 739–792). Both sides, for example, had abandoned the harsh and sometimes inflammatory rhetoric that had characterized relations since the Soviet invasion of Afghanistan. Beginning in 1986, superpower summits became an annual event, supplemented by increasingly frequent public and private contacts between senior-level policymakers (Schultz, 1993). Moreover, the United States and the Soviet Union were engaged in a set of diplomatic negotiations that held out the promise of far-reaching agreements in the realm of both arms control and regional conflict resolution.[14]

Despite these encouraging signs, however, relatively few concrete accomplishments had been realized by the time Ronald Reagan left office. This is not to discount the importance of the 1987 INF (intermediate range nuclear forces) treaty, which abolished intermediate and short-range missiles armed with nuclear warheads; nor is it to dismiss the significance of the Geneva agreement, which paved the way for the Soviet Union's withdrawal from Afghanistan. At the time, both of these breakthroughs were impressive achievements. This should be acknowledged, but at the same time we should not exaggerate the significance of these agreements.

Neither treaty, for example, dealt directly with the fundamental conflict of interest that had divided the United States and the Soviet Union since the end of World War II. This dispute, of course, centered on the political, military, and economic polarization of Europe. Since the late 1940s, Europe had been divided into two competing blocs: a U.S.–led alliance among the states of Western Europe, and a Soviet-dominated sphere of influence in Eastern Europe. The key institutional manifestations of this Cold War order were: (1) the division of Germany into two sovereign states, (2) alliance polarization in the form of the North Atlantic Treaty Organization (NATO) versus the Warsaw Treaty Organization (WTO), and (3) the organization of Europe into rival and relatively exclusive economic blocs. As of the beginning of 1989, these essential structures of the Cold War order were still basically intact.

If the superpowers were going to fundamentally transform the nature of their relationship, revolutionary changes would have to occur in Europe. At the time, this point was not lost on observers. In an article published on the eve of Bush's inauguration, for example, Richard Nixon (1988–1989: 199) warned that "the causes of the cold war—Moscow's domination of Eastern Europe and aggressive foreign policies around the world—still endure." The former president called on the Bush administration to make Europe its top foreign policy priority and to negotiate a political settlement with the Soviets that would lead to the liberation of Eastern Europe. In Nixon's (1988–1989: 209) view, the Cold War had begun in this region of the world, and "it will not end until Moscow's satellites receive their independence."

Similar sentiments were expressed by Michael Mandelbaum, a political scientist who, at the time, was serving as the director of the Council on Foreign Relations' Project on East-West Relations.[15]

> The core of the cold war in Europe is Soviet domination of Eastern Europe. . . . Ending the cold war requires ending the Soviet threat to Western Europe which requires ending Soviet subjugation of Eastern Europe. . . . The principal requirement for the end of the cold war, in short, is self-determination for Eastern Europe. (Mandelbaum, 1989: 21)

Acting on this advice, however, was fraught with risks. To seek the liberation of Eastern Europe was to challenge the vital interests of a major military power that, historically, had never hesitated to use force to maintain its position in the region. U.S. policymakers had long been rhetorically critical of the Soviet Union's presence in Eastern Europe. In practice, however, the United States typically had done little to effectively challenge Soviet control in the region.

Indeed, some scholars argue that a tacit security regime had emerged between the superpowers in regard to this issue (Kanet, 1990). At the core of this modus vivendi stood an unspoken agreement to respect each other's spheres of influence within Europe (Gaddis, 1987: 48–71; Nye, 1987: 393). Hence, to seek the liberation of Eastern Europe risked not only provoking the Soviet leadership; it also could weaken a norm of behavior that presumably had served to stabilize U.S.–Soviet interactions at the heart of the most heavily militarized region of the world.

This point leads to one additional consideration. The Cold War was, in many respects, a paradox. The superpowers and their respective allies had assembled the most formidable military arsenals in the history of international politics. They had amassed these capabilities in the name of a security strategy (i.e., deterrence) that sought to avoid war through the ultimate threat of nuclear annihilation. In the midst of this heavily militarized and highly competitive environment, however, the members of the European states system—both East and West—had become the unexpected beneficiaries of an unrivaled period of peace and prosperity in Europe.

The post–World War II era constitutes the longest uninterrupted period of major-power peace in the history of international politics (Gaddis, 1987). Since the defeat of Nazi Germany, not a single war has occurred between or among any of the major powers of Europe. In fact, over the past five decades, there has been only one war (i.e., 1956, Russo-Hungarian) and but a single major military intervention (i.e., 1968, Czechoslovakia) on the Continent (Small and Singer, 1982: 91–95).[16] Despite its many perils, the Cold War era did stand as the most stable period in the history of the European states system (see Levy, 1983: 71–73).

Admittedly, this stability was purchased at a considerable cost to the countries of Europe and North America. The Cold War order was characterized by unprecedented levels of militarization that had unfortunate socioeconomic consequences for the states and societies of both blocs (Kennedy, 1987: 395–437). At the same time, however, warfare is almost always more costly and destructive in terms of human and material resources than is even a heavily armed peace. This is especially the case within the context of a nuclearized system. Thus, we should not underestimate the significance of the Cold War's association with the long postwar peace. While obviously repugnant in many respects, the Cold War order was not the worst of all possible outcomes (Mearsheimer, 1990).

An appreciation of this fact confronted the Bush administration with a dilemma. The challenge was to formulate an approach to the Soviet Union that was bold yet not unduly provocative. Somehow, U.S. strategy needed to combine elements of both revisionism and restraint. The trick, of course, was to formulate a policy that would challenge the status quo in Europe without sparking either a confrontation with the Soviets or the precipitous collapse of the institutional arrangements that had regulated European security affairs since the end of World War II.

The task was further complicated by the uncertainty surrounding the Kremlin's attitude toward changes in Eastern Europe. In 1988, for example, Mikhail Gorbachev had made contradictory statements in public about the Soviet Union's role in the region. During a state visit to Yugoslavia in March, Gorbachev had expressed his "unconditional respect" for the principle of noninterference in the internal affairs of that country as well as a more general commitment to "the independence of . . . socialist countries to define, for themselves, the paths of their own development" (quoted in Gati, 1988–1989: 104). Two months later, however, Gorbachev seemed to retreat from this position when he indicated to *Washington Post* reporters that past Soviet interventions in Hungary and Czechoslovakia had been justified.

By the end of the year, Gorbachev had returned to the themes he had sounded in Yugoslavia. During a major address before the United Nations General Assembly, Gorbachev reiterated his support for self-determination and the norm of noninterference in the internal affairs of other countries.[17]

> Everyone, and the strongest in the first instance, is required to restrict himself and to exclude totally the use of external force. . . . The compelling necessity of the principle of freedom of choice is also clear to us. . . . This objective fact presupposes respect for other people's views and stands, tolerance, a preparedness to see phenomena that are different as not necessarily bad or hostile and an ability to learn to live side by side while remaining different and not agreeing with one another on every issue. (Quoted in Schultz, 1993: 1107)

At the time, one analyst characterized the twists and turns of the Soviet leadership's public statements regarding Eastern Europe during 1988 in the following way:

> A cloud of uncertainty hangs over Soviet intentions. On the one hand, Gorbachev still approves of past Soviet interventions and he still speaks of protecting the region's "common interests." On the other hand, Eastern European officials . . . no longer take it for granted that, in a crisis, they should either expect or count on Moscow's fraternal assistance. (Gati, 1988–1989: 102–103)

This was the backdrop against which the Bush administration took office on January 20, 1989. Ronald Reagan had bequeathed "a legacy of promise" to his successor (Schultz, 1993: 1130), but it was unclear whether the United States could translate this inheritance into a set of tangible achievements that would fundamentally transform the nature of U.S–Soviet relations. To accomplish this goal, significant revisions would have to be made in the basic institutional foundation of the Cold War order. How far the Soviet leadership was willing to go in this direction was a question few were able to answer.

The Bush administration attempted to cope with this dilemma by adopting a two-track policy toward the Soviet Union. On the one hand, the United States would initiate a series of "limited, reversible probes" designed to test Gorbachev's willingness to accept changes in the status quo in Europe.[18] At the same time, however, policymakers also would endeavor to reassure the Kremlin that the United States would not seek to exploit these changes to unilateral U.S. advantage.[19] In this way, the Bush administration sought to promote change while also minimizing the risk of provoking a serious confrontation with the Soviet Union.[20]

The Bush administration began implementing this two-track policy toward the Soviet Union in the spring of 1989. U.S. efforts centered principally on the subject of conventional arms control in Europe and support for the burgeoning reform movements then under way in both Poland and Hungary. In combination, the initiatives were intended to mount a preliminary challenge to both the military and political status quo in Europe.

Dramatic reductions in the conventional forces fielded by both NATO and the Warsaw Pact were at the heart of the Bush administration's approach for two basic reasons. Such an achievement, of course, would diminish the threat that Warsaw Pact forces posed to the West. Perhaps more important, however,[21] massive conventional force reductions would entail a corresponding reduction in the Soviet Union's military presence in Eastern Europe, which, in turn, could serve to create a military environment in the region conducive to the process of liberalization in Poland, Hungary, and other countries of the Soviet bloc.[22]

While pursuing a conventional arms reduction agreement in Europe, the Bush administration also began to challenge the political status quo on the Continent. The opening gambit came in a major foreign policy address delivered by the president in Hamtramck, Michigan.

> Arms are a symptom, not a source, of tension. The true source of tension is the imposed and unnatural division of Europe. How can there be stability and security in Europe and the world as long as nations and peoples are denied the right to determine their own future? . . . The United States . . . has never accepted the legitimacy of Europe's division. We accept no spheres of influence that deny the sovereign rights of nations. . . . The cold war began in Eastern Europe, and if it is to end, it will end in this crucible of world conflict. (*AFP,* 1989: 318–319)

In the name of overcoming the polarization of Europe, Bush also announced that the United States was prepared to support the process of political and economic reform in Eastern Europe. Poland was to receive the lion's share of U.S. attention because "if Poland's experiment succeeds, other countries may follow" (*AFP,* 1989: 320). The president justified this approach by invoking a vision of a "Europe whole and free."

> The West can now be bold in proposing a vision of the European future. We dream of the day when there will be no barriers to the free movement of peoples, goods, and ideas. We dream of the day when Eastern European peoples will be free to choose their system of government and to vote for the party of their choice in regular, free, contested elections. And we dream of the day when Eastern European countries will be free to choose their own peaceful course in the world, including closer ties with Western Europe. And we envision an Eastern Europe in which the Soviet Union has renounced military intervention as an instrument of its policy—on any pretext. (*AFP,* 1989: 320)

As part of this presentation, however, Bush also was quick to point out that the Soviet Union itself would benefit from such changes in Europe.

> The Soviet Union should understand in turn, that a free, democratic Eastern Europe as we envision it would threaten no one and no country. Such an evolution would imply and reinforce the further improvement of East-West relations in all dimensions—arms reduction, political relations, trade—in ways that enhance the safety and well-being of all of Europe. (*AFP*, 1989: 320)

Conventional Forces in Europe (CFE) and the "Hamtramck concept" were the centerpieces of the strategy of revisionism and reassurance that the Bush administration embraced prior to the grand strategy of institutionalization. The timing of the latter, beginning with Baker's speech to the Berlin Press Club, can perhaps best be attributed to the fall of the Berlin Wall on November 9, 1989.

Beschloss and Talbott (1993: 132) report that George Bush reacted to the East German government's decision to allow its citizens to pass freely into West Germany by remarking: "If the Soviets are going to let the Communists fall in East Germany, they've got to be really serious—more serious than I realized." The comment suggests that Bush interpreted this development as an indisputable sign of Gorbachev's willingness to accept fundamental changes in the essential structures of the Cold War order. Conceptually, the breaching of the Berlin Wall seems to have been regarded by Bush and other members of the administration as an "irrevocable commitment" (Stein, 1991: 42–43) that unambiguously signaled the Soviet leadership's desire to overcome the political polarization that had characterized the European states system since the late 1940s.

This impression seems to have been reinforced during Bush's subsequent meeting with Gorbachev on December 2–3. Beschloss and Talbott (1993: 166–167) report that Bush returned from the Malta summit convinced that "Gorbachev would be a reliable partner . . . [whom] he could do business with." The president himself intimated as much during a press conference held at the conclusion of the summit: "While it is not for the United States and the Soviet Union to design the future for Europeans or for any other people, I am convinced that a cooperative U.S.–Soviet relationship can, indeed, make the future safer and brighter" (*AFP*, 1989: 385–386).

This account of the timing of the grand strategy of institutionalization, however, sheds little light on its content. The Bush administration could have reacted to the fall of the Berlin Wall in a number of different ways. To account for the approach the administration actually did take, we need to locate the ideas underlying the strategy within the context of the U.S. diplomatic tradition.

The Content of the Strategy

The ideas underlying the Bush administration's response to the revolutions of 1989—democratization, marketization, and regional integration—are familiar themes within the context of twentieth-century U.S. statecraft. Indeed, some historians argue that U.S. foreign policy makers have been systematically promoting these ideas since World War I in an ongoing attempt to construct a liberal-capitalist world order (Levin, 1968; Maier, 1981; Hogan 1984, 1987). Hence, one could account for the content of the grand strategy of institutionalization by simply pointing to this enduring pattern of U.S. strategic thought.

While this may help to account for the general thrust of the Bush administration's approach, it sheds little light on some of the details of the strategy. Why, for example, did the Bush administration insist upon a multilateral approach when it came to supporting the process of liberalization in Eastern Europe? This choice was not inevitable. In the 1920s, for example, U.S. foreign policy makers tended to exhibit a preference for a more bilateral approach when it came to promoting liberal values and institutions in Europe (Leffler, 1979). Moreover, this argument cannot account for why the Bush administration preferred to broaden and deepen the role played by existing international institutions instead of advocating the creation of new ones.

There are two perspectives that might help to explain these choices. One is rooted in the presumption that states are "habit-driven actors" (Rosenau, 1984). This would suggest that the Bush administration reacted to changes in the international environment by drawing upon a repertoire of problem-solving tools that had become institutionalized within the United States government during the post–World War II era. This would depict the grand strategy of institutionalization as a cybernetic-like, programmatic response, the content of which reflects those policy instruments that decisionmakers found to be the most familiar and, hence, readily accessible. The other approach, however, would suggest that the Bush administration's response was not simply an exercise in instrumental rationality. Seen from this perspective, the content of the strategy can be traced to the lessons U.S. foreign policy makers have learned about the intrinsic value of multilateralism and existing international institutions over the past five decades.

The plausibility of the habit-driven actor hypothesis stems from the unique way in which the Cold War order collapsed. In the past, revolutionary geopolitical changes in Europe always had been occasioned by the outbreak of a catastrophic war among the major powers (Dehio, 1962; Holsti, 1991). The Thirty Years' War, the Napoleonic Wars, and World Wars I and II stand as prime examples. Such conflicts traditionally served as catalysts of change by effectively destroying the institutional foundations of the existing order and redistributing power and influence among states (Gilpin, 1981). In this way, massive major-power wars have played a perversely functional role in the historical evolution of the European states system (Modelski and Morgan, 1985).

The collapse of the Cold War order was unprecedented in this regard. Beginning in 1989, a series of fundamental geopolitical changes occurred in Europe, and yet at no point did the major powers seem close to war. Indeed, not a single serious major-power crisis was associated with the process. Historically speaking, the collapse of the Cold War order was unique (Jervis, 1991–1992); the world's most formidable military powers engaged in a process of peaceful change (Carr, 1939: 208–223).

While this was obviously a welcome development, we should not underestimate the complications this posed for the statespeople who were forced to try to navigate these uncharted waters. Periods of revolutionary change can be conceptualized in terms of two distinct, yet interrelated, processes: (1) the destruction of the status quo, and (2) the construction of a new international order. In the past, massive wars have served as breakpoints that, in practice, disentangle and separate the processes of destruction and creation. Such conflicts basically decompose the process of revolutionary change into two discrete phases: winning the war, and then crafting a peace settlement that will serve as the constitutional foundation of the new order.

By compartmentalizing the process of change, prolonged periods of major-power war also provide governments with an opportunity to develop plans for reconstructing the postwar order. Following the outbreak of World War II, for example, the United States government immediately created a postwar planning process that would remain in place until the very end of the conflict (Burley, 1993: 130–131). This opportunity, however, was not present in the case of the Cold War order. No one foresaw the momentous changes that were about to unfold in Europe (Gaddis, 1992–1993). Hence, scholars and policymakers alike had given relatively little thought to the problems and choices that suddenly would be thrust before them. Governments, of course, are not known for their ability to innovate and quickly adapt to a set of rapidly changing international circumstances (Kissinger, 1956). This problem appears to be particularly acute within the context of democratic governments where a commitment to pluralism and the free exchange of ideas combine to produce a decisionmaking process characterized by fragmentation, overlapping jurisdictional boundaries, discordant voices, and the need for consensus (Friedberg, 1989).

On the basis of these considerations, it seems plausible to argue that the content of the grand strategy of institutionalization may have been primarily a consequence of the Bush administration's need to quickly respond to a series of unexpected developments. Put differently, the administration's emphasis upon multilateral efforts coordinated through NATO, CSCE, and the European Community may not have been the result of a deliberative process wherein the relative merits of alternative approaches were discussed systematically but, rather, a consequence of the fact that the United States had to make some kind of response to the fall of the Berlin Wall and needed to do so in a hurry. In essence, the content of the grand strategy of institutionalization could represent a sublime example of satisficing.

This interpretation, however, overlooks the obvious fact that the approach advocated by the Bush administration has a proven track record of success in Europe. Hence, the United States' response to the end of the Cold War in Europe may have been more than simply an exercise in instrumental rationality; the content of the grand strategy of institutionalization may well be a reflection of the intrinsic value U.S. foreign policy makers have come to attach to multilateral institutions.

Following the end of World War II, U.S. foreign policy sought to promote liberal principles of political association in the interstate system by creating an array of multilateral economic and security institutions. As Anne Burley (1993: 146) points outs, "the roots of contemporary multilateralism lie in one particular liberal state's vision of the world as a domestic polity, economy, or society writ large." Drawing upon lessons derived from the Great Depression and the international conflicts that occurred during the 1930s, U.S. foreign policy makers endeavored to promote global peace and prosperity by establishing multilateral institutions that would serve as "specialized administrative organizations" for the management of international economic, security, and social problems (Burley, 1993: 130).

The onset of the Cold War, of course, confined the United States' efforts to promote multilateralism largely to the western half of the Continent. Even so, the United States continued to pursue this approach in regard to the countries of Western Europe throughout the Cold War era. Over the past five decades, these initiatives have led to a series of remarkable transformations in the region. In essence, Western Europe has evolved into a pluralistic security community: a group of countries characterized by a form of state sociality in which governments do not engage in coercive diplomacy or use force vis-à-vis one another.

In light of this experience, it is perhaps not surprising that the Bush administration was quick to recommend applying the same basic strategy in regard to the eastern half of the Continent. Secretary of State Baker made this point explicit during a 1991 speech in Berlin:

> The integration of Western Europe within the EC [European Community]
> and NATO has virtually transcended all the old territorial disputes,

> irredentist claims, and ethnic grievances among and within its members. Euro-Atlantic integration has made it literally inconceivable that local-ized disputes could become a source for serious conflict. . . . If we are to ensure comparable levels of peace and prosperity for Europe as a whole, comparable structures should be introduced to shape and develop inter-dependence among these countries. (Baker, 1991b: 62)

Seen from this perspective, NATO, the European Community, and CSCE represent more than simply functional international organizations; they also stand as concrete manifestations of a distinctively American (i.e., liberal) approach to post–World War II international politics. Hence, there are good reasons to suspect that the content of the grand strategy of insti-tutionalization can perhaps best be explained on the basis of the Bush ad-ministration's desire to build upon five decades of successful Western ex-perience with the task of creating a liberal international society in Europe. As Patrick Morgan points out:

> What Western governments clearly have in mind today is applying the same formula for the same objectives in order to get the same results so as to resolve the same basic security problem. . . . This is to continue the erosion of old conflicts, prevent the emergence of new ones, and result in a pluralistic security community—making resort to force among the new participants as improbable as it has become among those in the West. (Morgan, 1993: 345–346)

The Clinton Administration

The Clinton administration has continued to adhere to the basic conceptual framework articulated by James Baker. While some modifications have been introduced, these are primarily adjustment changes "in the level of effort and/or in the scope of recipients" (Hermann, 1990: 5) rather than a fundamental redefinition of the means and ends of U.S. strategy in Europe. Indeed, the degree of continuity is remarkable. This section presents evi-dence in support of this claim.

As a presidential candidate, Bill Clinton continually stressed the secu-rity benefits that would stem from the spread of democracy. The following passage, for example, appeared in a major foreign policy speech that Clin-ton delivered at Georgetown University in December 1991. It was entitled "A New Covenant for American Security."

> Democracies don't go to war with each other. . . . Democracies don't sponsor terrorist acts against each other. They are more likely to be reli-able trading partners, protect the global environment and abide by inter-national law. Over time, democracy is a stabilizing force. It provides

non-violent means for resolving disputes. Democracies do a better job of protecting ethnic, religious and other minorities. And elections can help resolve fratricidal civil wars. (Clinton, 1991: 5)

Clinton expressed similar sentiments before a gathering of the Foreign Policy Association in New York. This time, however, Clinton (1992a: 8) stressed the need for "a global alliance for democracy as united and steadfast as the global alliance that defeated communism." He went on to suggest that "no national security issue is more urgent."

The spread of free institutions will make foreign rulers more accountable to their people and check tyranny and external aggression. As nations free their economies from bureaucratic control they will become productive enough to satisfy more of their material wants and rich enough to buy more American goods and services. (Clinton, 1992a: 10)

Since taking office, Bill Clinton has continued to emphasize this theme. Indeed, he and other members of the administration routinely characterize the promotion and consolidation of democracy as one of the "three pillars" of U.S. foreign policy (e.g., Clinton, 1993b: 5; Christopher, 1993e: 11). In his first appearance before the North Atlantic Council, for example, Secretary of State Warren Christopher (1993b: 54) reaffirmed the Bush administration's conviction that "Europe's long term security . . . requires that we actively foster the spread of democracy and market economies."

The most comprehensive and coherent public presentation of the Clinton administration's security strategy, however, can be found in a speech delivered by National Security Adviser Anthony Lake at the Johns Hopkins School of Advanced International Studies in Washington. In words reminiscent of James Baker, Lake declared:

The successor to a doctrine of containment must be a strategy of enlargement—enlargement of the world's free community of market democracies. . . . To the extent that democracy and market economies hold sway in other nations, our own nation will be more secure, prosperous and influential, while the world will be more humane and peaceful. (Lake, 1993: 41)

The internal architecture of the Clinton administration's strategy also bears a striking resemblance to the Bush administration's approach. It consists, first and foremost, of efforts to promote the democratization and marketization of state-society relations throughout Eastern Europe and the former Soviet Union. In Lake's view, the strategy will lead the United States to:

help democracy and markets expand and survive in other places where we have the strongest security concerns and where we can make the greatest difference. This is not a democratic crusade; it is a pragmatic commitment to see freedom take hold where that will help us the most. . . . The most important example is the former Soviet Union. . . . If we can support and help consolidate democratic and market reforms in Russia and the other newly independent states, we can help turn a former threat into a region of valued diplomatic and economic partners. . . . The new democracies in Central and Eastern Europe are another clear example, given their proximity to the great democratic powers of Western Europe. (Lake, 1993: 42)

Multilateral economic and security institutions also figure prominently in the Clinton administration's approach. As Lake explained,

It is beyond doubt that multilateral action has certain advantages: it can spread the costs of action, as in our efforts to support Russian reform; it can foster global support, as with our coalition in the Gulf War; it can ensure comprehensiveness, as in our export control regimes, and it can succeed where no nation acting alone, could have done so. . . . I would go further and state . . . that the habits of multilateralism may one day enable the rule of law to play a far more civilizing role in the conduct of nations, as envisioned by the founders of the United Nations. (Lake, 1993: 45)

The Clinton administration's commitment to multilateralism also is indicated by the emphasis policymakers attach to the concept of collective security. Whereas the Bush administration only hinted in this direction, Bill Clinton and his advisers have called explicitly for the creation of a viable system of collective security in order to deal with regional security concerns in Europe and elsewhere.

As a candidate, for example, Bill Clinton (1992a: 11) characterized the end of the Cold War as "a broader opportunity . . . to reinvent the institutions of collective security." Since that administration took office, however, Madeline Albright—the United States' Ambassador to the United Nations—has emerged as the president's principal spokesperson in regard to this issue. During an appearance before a joint session of Congress' subcommittees on European security and international organizations, Albright stressed the importance of establishing a viable system of collective security to cope with the demands of the post–Cold War era.

If you were to search for one term that best describes the challenge confronting the new era, it is "collective security." The security threat to America—a threat that only collective security can ultimately manage—is a world where weapons of mass destruction proliferate and ethnic and religious conflicts trigger massive refugee flows, enormous economic dislocations, unacceptable human rights atrocities, environmental catastrophes and the senseless killing and maiming of civilians. That world has already arrived. . . . The United States cannot possibly rise to this challenge without a viable system of collective security. . . . [Without it] the United States will stand exposed to an endless raid on its resources, its goodwill, its soldiers, and finally its territorial integrity or the territorial integrity of its allies. (Albright, 1993c: 65–66)

Similarly, during a speech before the Council on Foreign Relations in New York, Albright specifically linked multilateral security institutions to the administration's desire to create a "principled international community."

A central goal of this administration is therefore to help create safeguards for a principled international community. . . . So, we in the United States must work energetically to strengthen the capacity of the United Nations and other multilateral organizations to conduct peacekeeping, preventive diplomacy, peacemaking, peace enforcement, humanitarian security and similar operations. . . . Rules aren't rules if they're not enforced. This does not require that we serve as the world's policeman, only that there should be policemen and that we take a hand in assuring their effectiveness. (Albright, 1993a: 34)

The difference between the Bush and Clinton administrations when it comes to collective security, however, is more a matter of style than of substance. The principle of collective security was also at the core of George Bush's vision of the "New World Order" emerging from the ashes of the Cold War. Consider, for example, the following comments that Bush made during a speech at Maxwell Air Force Base on April 13, 1991:

Twice this century, a dream born on the battlefields of Europe died after the shooting stopped. The dream of a world in which major powers worked together to ensure peace. . . . [The new world order] refers to new ways of working with other nations to deter aggression and achieve stability, to achieve prosperity, and, above all, to achieve peace. It is based on a shared commitment to four principles: peaceful settlement of disputes, *solidarity against aggression,* reduced and controlled arsenals, and the just treatment of all peoples. (Bush, 1991a: 32; emphasis added)

Bush returned to this theme during his 1992 farewell address to the United Nations General Assembly:

We have a unique opportunity . . . to forge . . . a genuine global community of free and sovereign nations—a community built on respect for principle, of peaceful settlement of disputes, fundamental human rights, and the twin pillars of freedom; democracy and free markets. . . . Meeting these challenges will require us to strengthen our collective engagement. It will require us to transform our collective institutions. . . . I welcome the Secretary-General's call for a new agenda to strengthen the United Nations' ability to prevent, contain, and resolve conflict across the globe. (Bush, 1992b: 59–60)

Democratization, marketization, and regional integration: These are the ideas that stand at the core of the Clinton administration's approach to post–Cold War Europe, just as they did for the Bush administration. It is on the basis of this indisputable pattern of convergent elite policy statements regarding the means and ends of U.S. foreign policy in Europe that we can feel confident in concluding that U.S. foreign policy makers have responded to the end of the Cold War in Europe by formulating a long-term program of action that can best be characterized as a grand strategy of institutionalization.

Conclusion

The evidence presented in this chapter was intended to: (1) document the emergence of the grand strategy of institutionalization in 1989–1990, (2) specify the internal architecture of the strategy, (3) document the Clinton administration's subsequent embrace of the strategy, and (4) present a preliminary explanation for both the timing and the content of the strategy. This has been done primarily through an analysis of documents released by the United States government.

The evidence suggests that U.S. foreign policy makers have responded to the end of the Cold War in Europe by formulating a grand strategy designed to facilitate far-reaching changes in the nature of the European states system. The strategy consists of distinct, yet mutually reinforcing, political, economic, and military initiatives oriented around the overarching goal of promoting and consolidating the spread of liberal norms and institutions throughout the Continent.

In practice, the grand strategy of institutionalization seeks to replicate, on a continental scale, the remarkable transformations that occurred in Western Europe during the Cold War. Ultimately, it is designed to facilitate the emergence of a liberal international society in Europe that will lead to enduring peace and prosperity throughout the Euro-Atlantic region.

Notes

1. This definition builds on the notion of grand strategy advanced by Deibel (1992: 40–41).

2. The analytic framework is similar in this regard to Robert Axelrod's (1976) well-known work on cognitive mapping. Instead of focusing on the structure of individual belief systems, however, the present study addresses the internal architecture of a state's security strategy.

3. This problem has long plagued the revisionist school of U.S. foreign policy studies. These scholars typically posit the existence of U.S. grand strategy on the basis of their understanding of the reproductive requirements associated with a capitalist economy. For a recent example of this scholarship, see McCormick (1989). A critique of the study, and revisionism in general, can be found in Gaddis (1990).

4. There are relatively few secondary sources currently available on the Bush administration. Moreover, most of these studies focus primarily upon the United States' involvement in the Gulf War and/or Bush's call for a "New World Order" (e.g., Tucker and Hendrickson, 1992). While these matters are not irrelevant to the issues raised here, they also do not speak directly to the United States' strategy toward post–Cold War Europe. At present, the best secondary source on the Bush administration's response to the collapse of the Soviet Union is Beschloss and Talbott's (1993) *At the Highest Levels.* This source, however, plays a relatively modest role in the present analysis. In general, the book simply tended to corroborate conclusions I already had drawn from my examination of the primary materials mentioned above. By cross-referencing the information contained in this book with the primary materials obtained from the United States government, my confidence in the soundness of the interpretation presented here has been enhanced considerably.

5. James Baker has signed a contract to publish his memoirs; George Bush and Brent Scowcroft are collaborating on a book that is scheduled for release in 1995.

6. One, of course, could interview individuals who have participated in the decisionmaking process relating to the United States' strategy toward post–Cold War Europe. This tack has a well-known number of problems associated with it, however. From a methodological standpoint, interviews raise as many questions about reliability and validity as do publicly available documents.

7. Obviously, this two-step analysis will diminish, but not totally eliminate, the risk of arriving at spurious conclusions concerning the existence and/or content of a state's grand strategy. Given the data limitations noted above, however, there are few alternative sources of information that presently could be used to test the interpretation advanced in this chapter. As additional archival materials become available, researchers will have an opportunity to bring this data to bear on the present analysis.

8. East German authorities opened the Berlin Wall on November 9, 1989. Over the next four months, Baker discussed the future of U.S. policy in Europe during major speeches in Berlin (December 12), Brussels (December 15), Prague (February 7), and Dallas (March 30).

9. The quote here is by George Bush, and it appears on page 297 of the 1989 *American Foreign Policy: Current Documents,* an annual State Department publication (Washington, D.C.: Government Printing Office). Hereafter, this source will be cited as *AFP,* followed by the year of publication.

10. In structuring this portion of the analysis around two of Baker's more noteworthy speeches, I am adhering to a precedent established in many previous studies of U.S. grand strategy. It is not unusual for political scientists to focus upon a rather small number of especially significant documents (e.g., Kennan's long telegram, *NSC* 68) when presenting the results of this type of analysis. This approach is warranted because, typically, the goal of such studies is to outline the essential features of U.S. policy rather than to provide a comprehensive account of the available diplomatic record. For our purposes, Baker's speeches to the Berlin Press Club and the World Affairs Council are useful because they provide a relatively concise and comprehensive overview of the overarching strategic design that senior-level members of the Bush administration would continue to emphasize throughout the remainder of their time in office.

11. This point also was affirmed publicly by President Bush during his State of the Union address on January 31, 1990. Appearing before a joint session of Congress and a national television audience, Bush declared that

the revolutions of 1989 have been a chain reaction, changes so striking that it marks the beginning of a new era in the world's affairs. . . . Our aim must be to ensure democracy's advance, to take the lead in forging peace and freedom's best hope: a great and growing commonwealth of free nations. (*AFP*, 1990: 1–2)

12. Baker made the same basic points during a February 7, 1990, speech at Charles University in Prague:

[G]overnments based on the consent of the governed are the first requirement for an enduring peace in Europe . . . because the principle of self-determination is the only basis upon which legitimate governments can stand. . . . Governments accountable to their people . . . will secure a Europe whole and free in a way armies of tanks never could. Democratic governments are far more likely to promote the well-being of their citizens than to pursue expansionist, aggressive aims. (*AFP*, 1990: 318–319)

13. The United Nations did not figure prominently in the Bush administration's public discussions of European security affairs, and of the grand strategy of institutionalization, until after the Gulf War. Thereafter, George Bush frequently emphasized the contribution the UN could make in the realm of international security management. This theme has become even more pronounced since President Clinton took office. I discuss the United Nations, and its role in U.S. strategy, below.

14. The reference here is to the Strategic Arms Reduction Talks and negotiations relating to the settlement of conflicts in Central America, Southern Africa, and Southeast Asia.

15. The Council on Foreign Relations is the premier foreign policy association of the Eastern establishment. A brief history of the council can be found in Hyland (1992).

16. The wars involving Bosnia, Serbia, and Croatia are interpreted here as a post–Cold War phenomenon. For present purposes, the temporal domain of the Cold War stretches from the end of World War II to the dissolution of both the Warsaw Treaty Organization and the Council for Mutual Economic Assistance in the spring of 1991.

17. During the address, Gorbachev also announced unilateral arms reductions that would entail the demobilization of 500,000 men and 10,000 tanks on the part of Soviet military forces.

18. The use of limited reversible probes is a tactic that governments can employ to test another state's commitment to defend the status quo. This approach is attractive because it enables a challenger to initiate change while also minimizing the risk of provoking a serious confrontation; it also is particularly useful when a state is uncertain about how an adversary will react to a challenge to the status quo (see George, 1991: 381).

19. A strategy of reassurance stands as a natural complement to the tactic of limited, reversible probes. In essence, a reassurance strategy seeks to reduce the likelihood of conflict by signaling a government's intention to exercise restraint vis-à-vis an adversary (Stein, 1991: 31–38). The goal is to diminish an adversary's concerns that its weaknesses, vulnerabilities, and/or concessions will be exploited by others for unilateral advantage. In this way, a reassurance strategy can encourage an adversary to accept changes in the status quo that otherwise might be unacceptable. This strategy is particularly useful for states whose relationship has been characterized by decades of mutual hostility and mistrust (Stein, 1991: 33). Within the context of an enduring rivalry, a strategy of reassurance can facilitate a process of reciprocal tension reduction whereby adversaries can minimize the risk of misperception and miscalculation, build confidence in one another's intentions, and gradually redefine the way they relate to, and interact with, one another (Stein, 1991: 33).

20. While this cautious approach can be attributed to the systemic context that confronted U.S. policymakers, it also may have been a product of George Bush's own personal political philosophy. According to Duffy and Goodgame, Bush is characterized by a deeply conservative worldview grounded in a set of fundamental doubts about the ability of government to shape the course of social and political events.

> Bush is . . . deeply skeptical of attempts by government to force the pace of human progress. Such efforts, Bush believes, are the height of hubris and folly and often bring unintended consequences. He believes that progress comes, when it comes, through glacial changes in attitudes. . . . Out of this skepticism of government grows a deep caution and fear of mistakes that Bush often expresses . . . as an overriding concern to "first, do not [sic] harm" and "not make things worse." Bush exhibits what management gurus decry as a "bias for inaction." . . . When he does move it usually is in reaction to someone else's initiative—and there he excels. His reflexes, instincts, and tactical skills are first-rate. (Duffy and Goodgame, 1992: 65)

21. Obviously, we should not exaggerate the immediate operational significance of the reductions proposed by the United States and NATO. Given the Soviet Union's overwhelming conventional military advantage relative to the states of Eastern Europe, the Red Army would have remained quite capable of intervening throughout the region even after an agreement had been signed. Symbolically, however, the Soviets' willingness to reduce their military presence in the East would stand as an encouraging sign of the Kremlin's desire to downplay the role of force as an instrument of its foreign policy.

22. This point was implicit in Baker's address at the opening of the Conventional Forces in Europe (CFE) negotiations in Vienna on March 6, 1989.

> We shall never be able to set East-West relations on an irreversible course toward enduring improvement unless we deal with the huge conventional military imbalances in Europe. . . . It is this array of Soviet armed might that divides Europe against its will and holds European hopes hostage to possibly hostile Soviet intentions. (*AFP*, 1989: 272)

2

BUILDING A NEW SECURITY ARCHITECTURE IN EUROPE

The deductive logic underlying the grand strategy of institutionalization is persuasive. There are, for example, compelling reasons to believe that democratization on a continental scale would serve to stabilize and pacify the European states system (see Russett, 1993). Nor can one dispute the superior productivity and wealth-producing capacity of market-based economies. Moreover, the post–World War II era clearly testifies to the fact that multilateral institutions can function as effective tools for the management of international economic, social, and even security problems.

To be successful, however, a grand strategy must be capable of being translated into practice. The conceptual eloquence of a strategic design will be of little consequence unless it can be implemented within the context of concrete historical circumstances. Hence, establishing the desirability of a strategy is not enough; policymakers also must attend to its feasibility (George, 1989; Howard, 1991: 36).

In recognition of this, this chapter chronicles the initial steps U.S. foreign policy makers have taken to implement the grand strategy of institutionalization. The analysis centers principally on the United States' efforts to construct a new architecture for European security. These overtures have consisted of: (1) a series of arms control initiatives designed to diminish the level of militarization on the Continent and to heighten the degree of military transparency between and among states; (2) an ongoing effort to develop a "strategic partnership" with Russia; and (3) a variety of proposals that would serve to broaden and deepen the role international institutions play in the management of regional security affairs.

While implementing the grand strategy of institutionalization clearly entails considerably more than simply building a new security architecture in Europe, no task is more pressing within the context of the United States' strategy. As indicated below, U.S. foreign policy makers are striving to fill the security vacuum created by the collapse of the Cold War order by expanding the role multilateral regimes play in the European states system. The success of this enterprise, in turn, holds important implications for the long-term success of the grand strategy of institutionalization. The following section elaborates on this point.

The Security Problematique

To build a liberal international society in Europe, simultaneous political and economic revolutions will have to occur in about two dozen countries located throughout the eastern half of the Continent. This transformative process will entail replacing highly centralized political and economic structures with more liberal institutions. It also will involve fundamental normative changes in the way hundreds of millions of people think about politics and markets. In practice, the grand strategy of institutionalization represents an exercise in social engineering that will require the nations and states of Eastern Europe to redefine their identities, interests, institutions, and principles of international political association.

Obviously, this transformative process will take years, if not decades, to complete. Democratization and marketization are evolutionary phenomena that literally take time to grow and develop (Huntington, 1991). Hence, the emergence of a true liberal international society in Europe lies some distance in the future. At present, the European states system can best be characterized as being in the midst of a transitional stage that, in principle, could lead in any one of a number of different directions.

For the rest of this decade, and perhaps beyond, the countries of Eastern Europe and the former Soviet Union will be faced with the formidable task of restructuring the nature of their state-society relations on the basis of liberal norms and institutions. Previous research indicates that such "weakly institutionalized liberal regimes" are especially vulnerable to international economic shocks and regional developments that heighten national security concerns (Snyder, 1989: 6–7). This implies that the United States and its allies can make an important contribution to the process of liberalization in Eastern Europe by: (1) maintaining the relative openness and stability that has characterized the capitalist world economy in the post–World War II era, and (2) establishing new regional security arrangements capable of managing the domestic and international conflicts that may arise during this lengthy transformative process (Snyder, 1990: 31–38; Van Evera, 1990–1991: 50–57).

The importance of the latter point is underscored by a recent empirical study that finds that new democracies are more likely to become involved in international conflict than are long-established democracies. As the authors point out, the results of the analysis suggest that

to the extent that norms and institutions take time to develop, newly created democracies in Eastern Europe and elsewhere may still experience
some significant amount of interstate conflict while their political systems are in the process of transition to democracy. (Maoz and Russett,
1993: 636)

The political geography of Eastern Europe reinforces the potential importance of this point. There are approximately twenty states currently undergoing simultaneous political and economic revolutions in Europe.
These countries also tend to be packed into a relatively confined geopolitical space extending from Poland to Russia and from Estonia to the former
Yugoslavia. Hence, a number of these countries share contiguous borders.

Researchers have found that contiguity can serve as a transmission
belt, diffusing conflict from one state to another (Most and Starr, 1980;
Starr and Most, 1983). This suggests that Eastern Europe may be especially prone to contagion effects that increase the likelihood that conflicts
will escalate horizontally. This also is likely to exacerbate the security
concerns of states located in the area. As indicated above, insecurity can
serve to complicate, retard, and perhaps even derail the reform process in
"weakly institutionalized liberal regimes."

This is a highly salient problem in Eastern Europe because the dissolution of the Soviet Union has precipitated the collapse of the international
arrangements that had served to regulate security issues in this part of Europe since the end of World War II. The Soviet Union's sphere of influence in the region and the Warsaw Treaty Organization both have been
swept away by the revolutionary forces unleashed by Mikhail Gorbachev's
"New Thinking." This, in turn, has led to the emergence of a type of institutional vacuum in the eastern half of the Continent, a geopolitical zone
of uncertainty and ambiguity concerning the rights and responsibilities of
states. As Stephen Van Evera points out, it is not uncommon for international conflict to emerge under such circumstances.

Peace among states is most durable when spheres of influence, the "rules
of the game," and the rights and responsibilities of all parties are clear.
Dangers rise when they are ambiguous; each state then tends to define its
own rights broadly and others' narrowly, and to dispute the others' definitions. Crises erupt as states issue threats and stage fait accomplis to
force others to accept their own definition of their rights. (Van Evera,
1990–1991: 45)

U.S. policymakers clearly are sensitive to this problem. Toward the
end of his presidency, for example, George Bush (1992b: 60) characterized regional violence as "the greatest threat to the democratic peace we
hope to build with Eastern Europe, with Russia and Eurasia, even more so

than economic deprivation." Similarly, in a speech to the UN General Assembly, President Clinton emphasized the importance of addressing the issue of Eastern European security:

> If we do not strengthen the capacity to resolve conflict among and within nations, those conflicts will smother the birth of free institutions, threaten the development of entire regions and continue to take innocent lives. (Clinton, 1993c: 51)

Since the late 1980s, U.S. foreign policy makers have attempted to address these concerns by: (1) promoting arms control agreements that would diminish the level of militarization in the region and heighten the degree of military transparency between and among states; (2) nurturing a "strategic partnership" with Russia; and (3) broadening and deepening the role international institutions play in the management of regional security affairs. The remainder of the chapter chronicles the steps the United States has taken in each of these directions.

Arms Control

U.S. arms control efforts in Europe have centered on three basic goals: (1) achieving significant conventional force reductions, (2) preventing the proliferation of nuclear weapons within the Continent, and (3) establishing confidence-building measures to increase military transparency. This section examines the progress the United States has made in each area.

Conventional Force Reductions

As mentioned in the previous chapter, the Conventional Forces in Europe (CFE) negotiations were a key component of the strategy of revisionism and reassurance pursued by the Bush administration during most of its first year in office. In 1990, these efforts came to fruition as the members of NATO and the WTO met in Paris to conclude an agreement that would lead to unprecedented conventional arms reductions throughout the Continent.

The CFE treaty was signed on November 19, 1990, by the states comprising NATO and the WTO. A central goal of the negotiations was to achieve "significant reductions in key military capabilities that are designed for invasion" (*AFP*, 1989: 270; quote by Baker). To this end, the treaty limits five categories of military hardware that are especially useful for large-scale offensive operations: tanks, armored combat vehicles, artillery, attack helicopters, and combat aircraft. The treaty allots each signatory a specific national "entitlement" for each type of treaty-limited equipment (TLE). These ceilings represent the legally binding, maximum holdings a state may possess in each category once the treaty is fully implemented (see *Arms Control Today*, 1991).

National entitlements were established on the basis of intra-alliance discussions. As alliances, NATO and the WTO both were allowed to possess the same amount of TLE: 20,000 tanks; 30,000 armored combat vehicles; 20,000 artillery pieces; 2,000 attack helicopters; and 6,800 combat aircraft. The members of each alliance were then permitted to decide how their overall allotment would be distributed among themselves. The only constraint on the resulting distribution was the so-called sufficiency principle: No single member of an alliance would be permitted to hold more than two-thirds of the alliance-wide total in each category (Dean and Forsberg, 1992: 82).

The CFE treaty was not affected by the dissolution of the WTO on March 31, 1991. Since each state had signed the agreement individually, the abrogation of the Treaty of Warsaw did not change their legal obligations under the terms of the CFE treaty. The dissolution of the USSR, on the other hand, necessitated a series of negotiations to determine how the Soviet Union's entitlements would be distributed among the successor states. This matter was finally resolved in May 1992 at a summit involving Russia and the other republics of the former Soviet Union.

The Tashkent Declaration apportioned the Soviet Union's entitlements under the treaty among Russia and other members of the Commonwealth of Independent States on the basis of a complicated formula that included the geographical extent of the respective states, the length of their borders, and the size of their populations (International Institute for Strategic Studies [hereafter IISS], 1992: 240–241). On average, Russia acquired approximately 50 percent of the Soviet Union's entitlements; Ukraine and Belarus received roughly 25 and 10 percent, respectively. In combination, these three states account for over 90 percent of TLE holdings allotted to the Soviet Union under the terms of the CFE treaty.

While engaged in the CFE negotiations, the Bush administration also proposed significant reductions in the number of military personnel that the United States and the Soviet Union could deploy in Europe. The United States' opening gambit in regard to this initiative came in May 1989. During a NATO summit in Brussels, President Bush proposed that the superpowers limit their military deployments in Europe to 275,000 soldiers. In his 1990 State of the Union address, Bush advocated even greater reductions suggesting that the superpowers diminish their military presence in the Continent to no more than 195,000 troops.

Following the completion of the CFE treaty, members of NATO and the WTO held a series of discussions in regard to this initiative. On July 10, 1992, these states issued a joint declaration concerning the deployment of military personnel in Europe. The CFE-1A agreement, known formally as the Concluding Act of the Negotiation on Personnel Strength of Conventional Armed Forces in Europe, constitutes a nonbinding commitment on the part of the signatories to limit their manpower deployments in the area covered by the CFE treaty.

The agreement consists of each government's declaration concerning the maximum number of military personnel it plans on deploying in Europe. Unlike the CFE treaty, the ceilings codified in the CFE-1A agreement were not subject to negotiation; rather, each state was responsible for determining its own personnel ceiling.[1] While technically the limits are nonbinding, the agreement does obligate each government to notify the other signatories before it exceeds the ceiling contained in the agreement. Moreover, each state has pledged to provide the other participating states with forty-two-days' advance notice before it increases the strength of any ground force by more than 1,000 men or calls up more than 35,000 reservists (Fitzwater, 1992b: 45).

The CFE treaty is to be fully implemented by January 17, 1996; the ceilings specified in the CFE-1A agreement are to be met by November 17, 1995. In combination, these agreements will yield the distribution of conventional military capabilities listed in Table 2.1.

Both the CFE treaty and the CFE-1A agreement are of unlimited duration. Hence, in principle, the hardware and personnel ceilings specified in the documents are to remain in place forever. At the time, James Baker (*AFP*, 1990: 286, 288) characterized these agreements as an attempt to "lock-in a new post–cold war military order" that would facilitate "the construction of a new, more stable, and legitimate European order."

Compared with the conventional force deployments that characterized the European states system throughout much of the Cold War era, the CFE and CFE-1A agreements clearly represent unprecedented reductions in the level of militarization on the Continent. Notice, however, that these agreements also institutionalize an overwhelming Russian advantage when it comes to the number of conventional forces that states may deploy in the region.

The magnitude of Russia's position relative to others can be seen more clearly by calculating the percentage shares of aggregate military capabilities that will be held by each of the participating states once the agreements are fully implemented. We arrive at this figure through the two-step process outlined in Singer, Bremer, and Stuckey (1972). First, the percentage share allotted to each country in terms of manpower and each category of TLE is determined. Then sum each country's percentage shares across these categories and divide by the total number of categories. The result is a positional picture of how conventional military capabilities will be distributed across these twenty-six states by the beginning of 1996. Table 2.2 reports the percentage shares for each signatory in each category as well as the aggregate percentage of military capabilities to be held by each state.

**Table 2.1   CFE and CFE-1A Ceilings
(to be met by January 17, 1996)**

State	Manpower	Tanks	ACV[a]	ART[b]	Hel.[c]	AC[d]
Russia	1,450,000	6,400	11,480	6,415	890	3,450
Ukraine	450,000	4,080	5,050	4,040	330	1,090
Belarus	100,000	1,800	2,600	1,615	80	260
Moldova		210	210	250	50	50
Armenia		220	220	285	50	100
Azerbaijan		220	220	285	50	100
Georgia		220	220	285	50	100
Poland	234,000	1,730	2,150	1,610	130	460
Romania	230,248	1,375	2,100	1,475	120	430
Czech.	140,000	1,435	2,050	1,150	75	345
Bulgaria	104,000	1,475	2,000	1,750	67	235
Hungary	100,000	835	1,700	810	108	180
Turkey	530,000	2,795	3,120	3,523	43	750
Germany	345,000	4,166	3,446	2,705	306	900
France	325,000	1,306	3,820	1,292	352	800
Italy	315,000	1,348	3,339	1,955	142	650
Spain	300,000	794	1,588	1,310	71	310
Britain	260,000	1,015	3,176	636	384	900
U.S.	250,000	4,006	5,372	2,492	518	784
Greece	158,621	1,735	2,534	1,878	18	650
Netherlands	80,000	743	1,080	607	69	230
Portugal	75,000	300	430	450	26	160
Belgium	70,000	334	1,099	320	46	232
Denmark	39,000	353	316	553	12	106
Norway	32,000	170	225	527	0	100
Canada	10,660	77	277	38	13	90

Source: IISS (1992: 244).
Note: As of this writing Moldova, Armenia, Azerbaijan, and Georgia had not declared their personnel ceilings.
a. ACV = armored combat vehicles.
b. ART = artillery.
c. Hel. = attack helicopters.
d. AC = combat aircraft.

The table indicates that Russia will possess a more than 2:1 advantage over its next nearest competitors (i.e., the United States and Ukraine) when it comes to conventional military strength in Europe. Russia's advantage relative to Germany, France, Britain, and Italy will be on the order of 4:1. The greatest power imbalances, however, will exist in regard to the Baltic States and the countries comprising Eastern Europe. In each case, Russia

**Table 2.2   Distribution of Conventional Military Capabilities
(percentage shares to be held by individual countries by 1996)**

State	Aggregate	Manpower	Tanks	ACV[a]	ART[b]	Hel.[c]	AC[d]
Russia	21.0	25.9	16.4	19.2	16.8	22.3	25.6
U.S.	9.5	4.4	10.2	8.8	6.5	13.0	5.8
Ukraine	8.9	8.0	10.4	8.4	10.6	8.3	8.1
Germany	7.4	6.2	10.6	5.8	7.1	7.7	6.7
Turkey	6.3	9.5	7.1	5.2	9.2	1.1	5.5
France	5.6	5.8	3.3	6.4	3.4	8.8	5.9
Britain	5.1	4.4	2.6	5.3	1.7	9.6	6.7
Italy	4.7	5.6	3.4	5.6	5.1	3.6	4.8
Poland	3.8	4.2	4.4	3.5	4.2	3.3	3.4
Greece	3.7	2.8	4.4	4.2	4.9	7.0	4.8
Romania	3.5	4.1	3.5	3.5	3.9	3.0	3.2
Belarus	3.1	1.7	4.5	4.3	4.2	2.0	1.9
Czech.	2.9	2.5	3.7	3.4	3.0	1.9	2.6
Spain	2.9	5.3	2.0	2.7	3.4	1.8	2.3
Bulgaria	2.8	1.9	3.8	3.3	4.5	1.7	1.7
Hungary	2.1	1.7	2.1	2.8	2.1	2.7	1.3
Netherlands	1.7	1.4	2.0	1.8	1.6	1.7	1.7
Belgium	1.4	1.3	>1.0	2.0	>1.0	1.2	1.7
Portugal	>1.0	1.3	1.0	>1.0	1.2	>1.0	1.2
Norway	>1.0	>1.0	>1.0	>1.0	1.4	>1.0	>1.0
Denmark	>1.0	>1.0	>1.0	>1.0	1.4	>1.0	>1.0
Armenia	>1.0	>1.0	>1.0	>1.0	1.3	>1.0	>1.0
Azerbaijan	>1.0	>1.0	>1.0	>1.0	1.3	>1.0	>1.0
Georgia	>1.0	>1.0	>1.0	>1.0	1.3	>1.0	>1.0
Moldova	>1.0	>1.0	>1.0	>1.0	1.4	>1.0	>1.0
Canada	>1.0	>1.0	>1.0	>1.0	>1.0	>1.0	>1.0

Source: Derived by author from data contained in IISS (1992: 244).
Note: In calculating the relative shares of personnel strength within Europe, Armenia, Azerbaijan, Georgia, and Moldova have been excluded from the analysis.
a. ACV = armored combat vehicles.
b. ART = artillery.
c. Hel. = attack helicopters.
d. AC = combat aircraft.

will hold at least a 6:1 advantage in the size of its relative conventional military capabilities.

For reasons suggested below, the United States has expressed relatively little concern about the power differentials institutionalized within Europe by the CFE and CFE-1A agreements. In essence, U.S. foreign policy makers believe that the democratization of Russia will mediate the strategic significance of these conventional force imbalances.

Preventing Proliferation

U.S. foreign policy makers have been aggressively promoting the norm of nuclear nonproliferation in Europe. The dissolution of the Soviet Union led to the emergence of four countries with strategic nuclear weapons located on their territories: Russia, Belarus, Ukraine, and Kazakhstan. In response to this, the United States has endeavored to persuade Belarus, Ukraine, and Kazakhstan to transfer these weapons systems to Russia and to sign the Nuclear Nonproliferation Treaty as non-nuclear weapon states. This policy was outlined by Secretary of State Baker in a major address delivered just four days after leaders from Russia, Belarus, and Ukraine issued a joint statement declaring "that the Union of Soviet Socialist Republics . . . is ceasing its existence."

> We do not want to see new nuclear weapons states emerge as a result of the transformation of the Soviet Union. . . . We also want to see Soviet nuclear weapons remain under safe, responsible, and reliable control with a single unified authority. . . . For those Republics who seek complete independence, we expect them to adhere to the Nonproliferation Treaty as non-nuclear weapon states, to agree to full-scope IAEA [International Atomic Energy Agency] safeguards, and to implement effective export controls in nuclear materials and related technologies. (Baker, 1991a: 20)

The strategic nuclear forces located in Russia, Belarus, Ukraine, and Kazakhstan constitute the most formidable long-range weapon systems ever produced by the Soviet Union. Table 2.3 provides an overview of the ballistic missile capabilities that devolved to these countries following the breakup of the Soviet Union. In addition to their ballistic missile inventories, Russia, Ukraine, and Kazakhstan also inherited long-range bombers capable of delivering nuclear weapons.[2] As of the time of the dissolution of the Soviet Union, Ukraine (1,662) and Kazakhstan (1,410) each possessed more strategic nuclear weapons than France, China, and Britain combined (i.e., 1,100 weapons).

To promote the denuclearization of Belarus, Ukraine, and Kazakhstan, the United States has resorted to both financial and diplomatic measures. On December 12, 1991, for example, Congress passed the Soviet Nuclear Threat Reduction Act (i.e., the Nunn-Lugar Act). The legislation established a $400,000,000 foreign assistance program for the express purpose of helping to dismantle the nuclear weapons of the former Soviet Union.

On May 23, 1992, the United States took another step in this direction by persuading Belarus, Ukraine, and Kazakhstan to sign the so-called Lisbon Protocol. The agreement established a legally binding commitment on

Table 2.3   ICBMs Inherited by the Successors to the Soviet Union

State	ICBM Type	Range (km)	Total No.	Warheads per Missile	Warhead Yield	CEP (m)
Russia	SS-11	13,000	280	3 x MIRV[a]	1MT[b]	1,100
	SS-13	9,400	40	single RV[c]	600KT[d]	1,800
	SS-17	10,000	40	4 x MIRV	500KT	400
	SS-18	9,000	204	10 x MIRV	500KT	250
	SS-19	10,000	170	6 x MIRV	500KT	300
	SS-24	10,000	46	10 x MIRV	100KT	200
	SS-25	10,500	260	single RV	750KT	200
Ukraine	SS-19	10,000	130	6 x MIRV	500KT	300
	SS-24	10,000	46	10 x MIRV	100KT	200
Kazakhstan	SS-18	9,000	104	10 x MIRV	500KT	250
Belarus	SS-25	10,500	80	single RV	750KT	200

Source: IISS (1992: 233).
Note: Circular error probability (CEP) is a measure of a missile's accuracy relative to an aim point. The figure indicates "the radius of a circle around a target within which there is a 50 percent probability that a weapon aimed at that target will fall" (IISS, 1992: 236).
a. MIRV = multiple independently targetable re-entry vehicles.
b. MT = megaton.
c. RV = re-entry vehicle.
d. KT = kiloton.

the part of these countries to pursue the path of nuclear disarmament. Under the terms of the protocol, "all nuclear weapons and all strategic offensive arms" located on their territories are to be "eliminated" by the end of the 1990s. Moreover, the signatories are obligated "to join the Nonproliferation Treaty in the shortest possible time." As the Bush administration explained on the day of the signing, the Lisbon Protocol "confirms and consolidates the non-nuclear status" of these states, leaving Russia as the only nuclear weapons state in Eastern Europe (Baker, 1992b: 54).

As with the CFE and CFE-1A agreements, the Lisbon Protocol represented an attempt to "lock in" another piece of Europe's post–Cold War military order. In this case, however, U.S. foreign policy makers were not looking to fundamentally change the situation that had prevailed in Europe since the 1960s. To the contrary, the Libson Protocol reflects the United States' underlying commitment to preserve the nuclear status quo in Europe by preventing any other states from joining the region's long-established nuclear powers.

As of this writing, both Belarus and Kazakhstan have acceded to the Nuclear Nonproliferation Treaty as non-nuclear weapon states. Ukraine, however, has been reluctant to agree to the elimination of all of the strategic nuclear weapons located on its territory. On November 18, 1993, for example, the Ukrainian parliament voted, 254 to 9, in favor of retaining 48 percent of the 176 ballistic missiles presently deployed in the country (Shapiro, 1993: A45). In January 1994, however, Ukraine did sign another agreement with the United States and Russia reaffirming its pledge to become a non-nuclear state by the end of the decade (Devroy, 1994: A1). As of this writing, however, Ukraine has yet to accede to the nonproliferation treaty.

Confidence-Building Measures

U.S. foreign policy makers have supplemented their conventional and nuclear arms control efforts by actively promoting confidence-building measures (CBMs) that will serve to increase the degree of military transparency between and among states. The presumption underlying CBMs is that transparency (i.e., openness) can help to reduce the potential for military confrontations while also building confidence in the benign intentions of former adversaries (Lamb, 1988: 42).

During the Bush administration's term, U.S. efforts centered principally on the so-called open skies initiative. This referred to a proposed multilateral arrangement whereby participating states would be permitted to conduct reconnaissance flights over one another's territories (*AFP*, 1989: 365). In James Baker's view, an open skies regime would strengthen European security because

> [u]nder [this] approach, states will be able to see more clearly—literally—the actions and intent of others, whatever the time of day, whatever the weather. A state will not be able to practice and exercise for offensive, aggressive attacks with the help of a traditional ally—a closed society. Neighbors will be able to fly over troop movements, lowering the possibility of surprise attack. And by improving assessments of a potential adversary's capabilities and likely intentions, Open Skies can reduce miscalculation and misperceptions—and in doing so, alleviate those fears that are oftentimes the source of escalating tensions. (*AFP*, 1990: 63)

This initiative ultimately met with success on March 24, 1992, when the United States, Russia, and twenty-two other countries signed the Open Skies Treaty in Helsinki. The agreement commits the signatories to "make all of their territory accessible to aerial observation." Moreover, each state is required to allow a fixed number of annual reconnaissance flights over its territory, the precise number to be determined on the basis of each participating state's geographic size. As the largest participants, both the United States and Russia are obligated to accept forty-two observation flights per year. The Open Skies Treaty also is to last in perpetuity and is open to accession by all states.[3]

Following the signing of the agreement, the Bush administration characterized the open skies regime as

> the most wide-ranging international confidence-building measure ever developed, covering the entire territory of North America and nearly all of Europe and the former Soviet Union. Its arrangements for observation flights . . . are innovative means to help promote openness and stability in Europe in these uncertain times. . . . The United States believes that the greater transparency in military activities brought about by such an agreement will help reduce the chances of military confrontation and build confidence in the peaceful intentions of the participating states. (Fitzwater, 1992a: 38)

The United States also has supported CBMs negotiated under the auspices of the CSCE. On November 19, 1990, for example, the United States and thirty-three other states signed the Concluding Document of the Vienna Negotiations on Confidence and Security Building Measures. The agreement commits the signatories to annual information exchanges concerning: (1) the content of their military budgets, (2) the planned deployment of major weapon systems, (3) the organization and deployment of military personnel, and (4) any military exercise involving more than 40,000 soldiers.[4]

U.S. efforts to enhance transparency also have been undertaken within the context of NATO and the North Atlantic Cooperation Council (NACC). Similarly, the United States has proposed a wide range of bilateral contacts with Russia in the name of nurturing greater military openness on the part of the superpowers. These initiatives are discussed below.

Conclusion

U.S. arms control efforts in Europe since the end of the Cold War have been driven by a desire to create a military environment "free of intimidation and the threat of invasion" (*AFP*, 1989: 273; quote by Baker). To this end, the United States has endeavored to establish regional arms control arrangements that would lead to: (1) significant reductions in the level of militarization within the Continent, and (2) greater military transparency between and among states. These initiatives have been supplemented by ongoing U.S. efforts to establish a new "strategic partnership" with Russia and to strengthen the role international institutions play in the management of regional security affairs. We turn now to a consideration of these efforts.

Developing a "Strategic Partnership" with Russia

In theory, the grand strategy of institutionalization is a global enterprise designed to facilitate the emergence of "market democracies" around the world. In practice, however, there is little doubt that democratization in Russia stands as the United States' number one strategic priority (see Baker, 1991a; Lake, 1993: 42; Christopher, 1993f).

Conceptually, U.S. policymakers have linked the success of Russian reform to four key U.S. interests. One of the most explicit discussions of this point can be found in a speech delivered by President Clinton to the American Society of Newspaper Editors on April 1, 1993. According to the president, the democratization of Russia will, first and foremost, enhance U.S. security by eliminating the risk of Russian aggression in Europe.

> Across most of our history, our security was challenged by European na-
> tions set on domination of their continent and the high seas that lie be-
> tween us. . . . Now, we could at last face a Europe in which no great
> power, not one, harbors continental designs. . . . The rise of a democra-
> tic Russia, satisfied within her own boundaries, bordered by other peace-
> ful democracies, could ensure that our nation never needs to pay that kind
> of price again. (Clinton, 1993d: 21)

A greatly diminished risk of Russian imperialism, in turn, will lead to additional benefits for the United States. It will, for example, enable the United States to forgo billions of dollars worth of defense expenditures, thus allowing these monies to be redirected to the task of rehabilitating its economy. Russian democratization also will create opportunities to expand Russo-American economic relations; this will translate into increased U.S. exports, more jobs, and continued economic growth (Clinton, 1993d: 21).

In addition, however, democracy in Russia will enable the United States to establish a "strategic partnership" with its former adversary: a co-operative relationship based upon a common commitment to "global problem solving" (Clinton, 1993d: 21). This is of considerable importance to U.S. foreign policy makers because Russo-American cooperation would seem to be a prerequisite for strengthening the role international institutions play in the management of international security issues in Europe and elsewhere. This section examines the steps U.S. foreign policy makers have taken to establish a strategic partnership with the Russian Federation.

The United States has approached this task by trying to establish a "basic political framework of relations" (George, 1988a: 667) with Russia. The vehicle for doing so has been a series of joint declarations that specify the principles and norms guiding their relationship in the realm of security. Substantively, these documents are analogous to the "basic principles agreement" that the United States and the Soviet Union concluded in 1972 (George, 1983: 107–116). In essence, U.S. foreign policy makers have promoted these agreements as an attempt to establish a normative framework that will shape the long-term evolution of Russo-American relations (Bush, 1992a: 18).

Three such documents have been signed since the beginning of 1992: the Camp David Declaration (February 1, 1992), the Charter for American and Russian Partnership and Friendship (also known as the Washington Charter) (June 17, 1992), and, most recently, the Vancouver Declaration (April 4, 1993). Of these, the Washington Charter provides the greatest insights into the nature of a strategic partnership between the United States and Russia.

The Charter for American and Russian Partnership and Friendship was signed by George Bush and Boris Yeltsin on June 17, 1992. The text: (1) specifies the basic principles underlying the countries' bilateral security relationship; (2) identifies the general goals and interests shared by the United States and Russia; and (3) provides the general outlines of a joint program of action that the two states will pursue in the realm of international security management.[5]

According to the Washington Charter, Russo-American relations are based upon three fundamental principles: First, the two countries no longer regard each other as adversaries; instead, relations are to proceed on the basis of "mutual trust and respect." Second, the United States and Russia also reject coercive diplomacy as an element of their bilateral relations. Put differently, the countries pledge "to settle disputes between them by peaceful means and to refrain from the threat or use of force against the territorial integrity and political independence of each other." Third, Russo-American relations also are based on the principle of indivisibility; both countries agree "that security is indivisible from Vancouver to Vladivostok." As a corollary to this principle, the document also affirms that the United States and Russia possess a "special responsibility . . . for maintaining international peace and security."

The text also specifies a set of goals and objectives that the United States and Russia share in regard to the international political system:

> The United States of America and the Russian Federation reiterate their determination to build a democratic peace, one founded on the twin pillars of political and economic freedom. . . . Beginning on the basis of their shared democratic values, the United States of America and the Russian Federation will unite in their efforts toward strengthening international peace and security, preventing and settling regional conflicts, and solving global problems. (*FBP*, 1992: 13)

In support of these goals, the Washington Charter outlines a series of steps that the United States and Russia will take in the area of international security management. The countries pledge, for example, to intensify their bilateral contacts in the name of "coordinating crisis prevention activities" and furthering "arms control and disarmament." The United States and

Russia are also committed to cooperation when it comes to strengthening "international means of collective engagement." Significantly, this commitment emerges within the context of a passage addressing the subject of European security.

> [The United States and Russia] cannot accept another phase of European instability. . . . Therefore, mechanisms for conflict prevention, management, and settlement and European peacekeeping must be strengthened if we are to adequately cope with future conflicts. To this end, the United States of America and the Russian Federation . . . support the strengthening of the Euro-Atlantic Community . . . [and] institutions like NACC, NATO, WEU [Western European Union] and CSCE. (*FPB*, 1992: 13)

Ultimately, the Washington Charter envisions "building a strategic partnership between the United States of America and the Russian Federation." Since taking office, the Clinton administration has continued to work toward this goal as well. The Vancouver Declaration, for example, reaffirms the Washington Charter as the "basis for relations between the two countries." The text also reiterates the superpowers' pledge to cooperate in the name of improving "the peacemaking and peacekeeping capabilities of the United Nations, the CSCE, and other appropriate regional organizations." To this end, the declaration also commits the United States and Russia "to broaden [their] interaction and consultations . . . in the areas of defense and security."[6]

A cooperative relationship with Russia is an essential component of the United States' strategy for strengthening the role international institutions play in the management of European security issues. The importance of this fact will become evident once we examine the practical steps U.S. foreign policy makers have taken to enhance the contribution international organizations can make in the realm of security.

International Institutions

Three institutions have figured most prominently in the United States' efforts to construct a new architecture for European security: CSCE, NATO, and the UN. While other international institutions (e.g., the European Community) clearly have important roles to play within the overall design of the grand strategy of institutionalization, U.S. foreign policy makers have tended to emphasize the potential value of CSCE, NATO, and the UN when it comes to the task of regional conflict management. This section chronicles the initiatives the United States has pursued in regard to each institution.

Conference on Security and Cooperation in Europe

CSCE is a multilateral institution whose origins can be traced back to the heyday of U.S.–Soviet détente during the 1970s (Gartoff, 1985: 106–121, 463–489). Since the inception of CSCE, its negotiations have been dedicated to the goal of establishing principles, norms, and rules that would serve to regulate East-West relations in the areas of military transparency, economic and commercial exchange, science, the environment, and human rights (Maresca, 1988: 106–107). At present, fifty-two countries are members of CSCE. This includes the United States, Canada, and every state located in Europe. As the only true Pan-European institution operative within the Continent, CSCE has been at the center of the United States' strategy since the very beginning of the post–Cold War era. Indeed, the United States has introduced more innovations in regard to CSCE than has any other existing institution.

As noted in the previous chapter, the Bush administration considered CSCE to be ideally suited to the task of promoting and consolidating democratic values and institutions in Eastern Europe and the former Soviet Union (*AFP*, 1989: 302–304; citing Baker). Moreover, U.S. foreign policy makers hoped that CSCE could make a direct contribution in the realm of international conflict management through its activities relating to confidence-building measures and the peaceful resolution of disputes.

Since 1989, U.S. foreign policy makers have consistently supported initiatives that would strengthen CSCE's ability to function in each of these areas. During a June 1990 address before the North Atlantic Council, for example, Secretary of State Baker outlined the United States' thinking in regard to the future of this institution.

> CSCE can serve the European common interest best by acting as a forum where the states of Europe discuss common problems and concerns. I've called it the "conscience of the continent," a place where the political and moral consensus of the time can be shaped based on democratic values. CSCE . . . [is] uniquely suited for building consensus to meet Europe's major challenges: ensuring political legitimacy . . . strategic stability and predictability. (*AFP*, 1990: 266)

Baker elaborated on this theme in October by proposing a number of specific steps that could be taken to "strengthen CSCE both politically and institutionally." The recommendations included: (1) a more regular process of consultation among member states; (2) the creation of a permanent secretariat; (3) the establishment of an "elections monitoring office"; and (4) the creation of a "conflict promotion center to promote confidence, predictability, and transparency through exchanges of military information and discussions of unusual military activities and to facilitate the conciliation of disputes" (*AFP*, 1990: 285).

In November 1990, CSCE members approved each of these proposals. The innovations are codified in the Charter of Paris for a New Europe, which was signed at the conclusion of the CSCE summit in France. The charter outlines an organizational structure designed to facilitate "the intensification of our consultations at all levels." To this end, CSCE members established both a permanent bureaucracy and several specialized functional offices.

The Council of Foreign Ministers will serve as "the central forum for political consultations within the CSCE process." It is to meet regularly and at least once a year. Ad hoc sessions in response to "emergency situations" also are contemplated. This body is to be assisted by a Committee of Senior Officials (CSO), who "will prepare the meetings of the Council and carry out its decisions." Administrative support for both the council and the CSO is to be provided by a secretariat located in Prague.

In addition, the charter also calls for the creation of three functional offices. A Conflict Prevention Center (CPC) is to be established in Vienna "to assist the Council in reducing the risk of conflict." An Office of Free Elections (OFE) will be set up "to facilitate contacts and the exchange of information on elections within participating States." Finally, the document also calls for the creation of a CSCE parliamentary assembly.

In subsequent meetings, CSCE members have built upon this basic institutional framework. On January 30, 1992, for example, state representatives agreed to enhance the jurisdictional scope of both the bureaucracy and the functional offices. The so-called Prague Document authorizes the council and the CSO to take action in response to "clear, gross, and uncorrected violations of relevant CSCE commitments . . . [even] in the absence of the consent of the state in question."[7]

This is a potentially important change because, previously, a government could prohibit CSCE involvement in its internal affairs by simply voting against such proposals. Historically, the CSCE decisionmaking process has operated on the basis of the unanimity principle (Maresca, 1985). Hence, in practice, each member has possessed a veto over CSCE activities. The Prague Document suspends this principle under the extraordinary circumstances suggested above.

Institutional innovations also were introduced in regard to the Conflict Prevention Center. The Prague Document establishes a Consultative Committee within the CPC, which is to serve as "a forum for consultation and cooperation in conflict prevention and for cooperation in the implementation of decisions on crisis management."

As part of this process, each member is encouraged to bring to the committee's attention any issue "which in its view has politico-military implications." Moreover, the committee is authorized to "execute factfinding missions" relevant to the task of preventing, managing, and resolving conflict. In the name of carrying out these activities, the Consultative Committee is to meet regularly, at least once a month.

CSCE's role in regard to international conflict management was further enhanced in July 1992. The "Final Act" of the Helsinki summit expands the jurisdictional scope of the institution further by reaffirming the principle that states are internationally accountable for their domestic human rights practices.

> We recognize our accountability to each other for complying with them [i.e., human rights standards]. . . . We emphasize that the commitments undertaken in the field of the human dimension of the CSCE are matters of direct and legitimate concern to all participating States and *do not belong exclusively to the internal affairs of the State concerned* [emphasis added].[8]

In keeping with this, the Final Act also calls upon the Council of Foreign Ministers to appoint a High Commissioner on National Minorities who will be authorized to investigate and help resolve minority problems "that have the potential to develop into a conflict within the CSCE area."

Perhaps more important, however, the Final Act also elaborates on the role CSCE can play within the context of European peacekeeping operations. This issue is addressed in a section entitled "CSCE and the Management of Change."

> CSCE peacekeeping activities may be undertaken in cases of conflict within or among participating States. Peacekeepers may supervise and help maintain cease-fires, monitor troop withdrawals, support the maintenance of law and order, and provide humanitarian and medical aid and assist refugees; they will not engage in peacemaking. CSCE peacekeeping requires the consent of the parties concerned . . . [and] will be initiated by consensus decision-making. (61)

The document also establishes a Forum on Security Cooperation (FSC), which will serve as "the sole forum for conventional arms control in Europe." The FSC's role is to facilitate dialogue pertaining to military issues, defense conversion, nonproliferation, regional disputes, CBMs, and arms control negotiations.

Following the completion of the Helsinki summit, Secretary Baker characterized the security-related provisions contained in the Final Act as "a four point structure to strengthen CSCE's ability to prevent crises and to manage crises that aren't prevented":

> There is a *first* early warning phase, which concentrates on human rights and democratic institution-building as a way to prevent conflicts before they develop. A *second* phase of political management focuses on steps

to encourage an end to conflicts. A *third* phase brings in specific instruments such as fact-finding missions and mechanisms for peaceful settlement of disputes. A *final* phase involves formal peacekeeping operations if all other efforts fail. (Baker, 1992a: 63)[9]

North Atlantic Treaty Organization

NATO is a multilateral institution composed of sixteen states. Its origins can be traced back to the North Atlantic Treaty signed on April 4, 1949. NATO is an alliance based upon the principle of collective security. Article 5 of the North Atlantic Treaty commits the signatories to regard an armed attack against any of the members as an attack against them all. Moreover, each member pledges to come to the assistance of allies under attack using "such action as it deems necessary, including the use of armed force." In principle, Article 5 constitutes an unconditional and legally binding commitment on the part of NATO's members to respond to any and all acts of aggression perpetrated against any one of the signatories from whatever quarter.

Since the end of the Cold War, U.S. foreign policy makers have consistently characterized NATO as an indispensable component of Europe's emerging security architecture (see, e.g., *AFP*, 1989: 296–298; *AFP*, 1990: 305–306; Clinton, 1992a). As noted previously, the United States has envisioned NATO playing a prominent role in facilitating an East-West dialogue in regard to both arms control and regional conflict management (*AFP*, 1989: 301; citing Baker).[10]

To fulfill this purpose, however, NATO would have to be adapted to the vicissitudes of the post–Cold War era. More than anything else, this would entail strengthening the alliance's "political dimension" (*AFP*, 1990: 252, 255). Secretary Baker elaborated on this point during a NATO ministerial meeting in June 1990.

> NATO cannot only prevent war but can also build peace. . . . The way to build peace is to reassure the Central and Eastern Europeans and the Soviets that they will not be left out of the new Europe. . . . One way we can do this . . . is through a solid dialogue and even regular consultations, both military and political. (*AFP*, 1990: 266)

A preliminary step in this direction was taken at the July 1990 NATO summit in London. Article 4 of the so-called London Declaration explicitly acknowledged NATO's changing role in Europe.

> In the new Europe, the security of every state is inseparably linked to the security of its neighbors. NATO must become an institution where Europeans, Canadians, and Americans work together not only for the common

defence, but to build partnerships with all the nations of Europe. The Atlantic Community must reach out to the countries of the East which were our adversaries in the Cold War, and extend to them the hand of friendship.[11]

To this end, the declaration also called for the creation of institutionalized diplomatic contacts between NATO and its former adversaries.

> To reflect the changing political role of the Alliance, we today . . . invite the U.S.S.R, Czechoslovakia, Hungary, Poland, Bulgaria, and Romania to come to NATO, not just to visit but to establish regular diplomatic liaison with NATO. This will make it possible for us to share with them our thinking and deliberations in this historic period of change. . . . We [also] are ready to intensify military contact . . . with Moscow and other Central and Eastern European capitals. (276)

A year later, this innovation was followed by a redefinition of NATO's overarching security strategy in Europe. The alliance's new "Strategic Concept" was unveiled at the conclusion of a NATO summit on November 8, 1991. According to the Rome Declaration, NATO's fundamental approach to European security would now consist of "three mutually reinforcing elements: dialogue; cooperation; and the maintenance of a collective defence capability."[12] As part of this strategy, the document also called for "a qualitative step forward" in terms of NATO's relationship with the states of Eastern Europe and the former Soviet Union.

To this end, the alliance outlined a series of proposals that would serve to develop "a more institutional relationship of consultation and cooperation on political and security issues." At the centerpiece of this initiative was a call for the establishment of a North Atlantic Cooperation Council: a forum that would facilitate regularized diplomatic contacts at the ministerial level.

The North Atlantic Cooperation Council (NACC) has become the principal NATO forum for East-West consultations and cooperation in the realm of security. In the view of Secretary of State Lawrence Eagleburger (1992: 116), NATO and the NACC constitute "the foundation of a truly European-wide security system."[13] In his farewell address to the NACC in December 1992, Eagleburger outlined the United States' aspirations in regard to the NACC and the future of European security.

> If the NACC, together with NATO, is to begin to realize its ultimate potential as a cornerstone of a European security system, it must develop a substantive agenda related to the real security challenges the new Europe faces today. . . . We think it is particularly important that we work closely within the NACC on planning, training, and other preparations for peacekeeping operations. . . . If the security interests of Europe East and West

are truly to become indivisible . . . we are all going to have to act as if this were the case by working together to confront threats to the peace and stability of this continent wherever they occur. . . . And as such habits and patterns of cooperation become ingrained, this could contribute to transforming the composition of the Alliance itself. (Eagleburger, 1992: 116)

This statement is significant in two respects. First, it reaffirms and broadens NATO's commitment to participate in European peacekeeping operations. Second, it raises the issue of expanding NATO's membership to include states located in Eastern Europe and the former Soviet Union. Both points deserve a brief discussion.

NATO's willingness to undertake peacekeeping missions in Europe was first articulated publicly in a communiqué issued on June 4, 1992: "We are prepared to support, on a case-by-case basis in accordance with our own procedures, peacekeeping activities under the responsibility of the CSCE, including by making available Alliance resources and expertise."[14] Eagleburger's statement, however, expands on this commitment by inviting Eastern European states to participate in peacekeeping operations under the auspices of the NACC. This invitation has been seconded by the Clinton administration. In a speech to NATO's foreign ministers, for example, Secretary of State Warren Christopher argued that

> We should intensify and expand the work program for the NACC and broaden its mandate. . . . The NACC states should step up joint consultations, joint activities on peacekeeping . . . and joint exercises. (Christopher, 1993c: 23)

In the name of developing "a joint capability to act together in future peacekeeping operations," the United States recently has decided to offer the Marshall Center in Garmisch, Germany, "as a forum and training center for NACC activities and other efforts to address the defense and security issues of the post–Cold War era" (Christopher, 1993a: 54). This proposal also is indicative of the Clinton administration's belief that

> The NACC is becoming a central element in the growing web of security ties that binds us together. It is tangible proof that the security of NATO members is linked to that of all states in Europe. . . . This sends a powerful signal of the resolve of the Euro-Atlantic community to respond effectively to new threats to peace, stability, and human rights. (Christopher, 1993a: 54)

Expanding NATO's membership to include the countries of Eastern Europe and the former Soviet Union has proven to be a more nettlesome problem for U.S. foreign policy makers. Since the dissolution of the Soviet

Union, several states have expressed an interest in becoming full-fledged members of NATO. They include, most prominently, Poland, Czechoslovakia, and Hungary. The alliance, however, has been reluctant to move in this direction presumably because of a concern that such a move would inflame the domestic political situation in Russia (Drozdiak, 1993: A25).

Incorporating Eastern European countries into NATO could provide fodder for nationalist groups and coalitions seeking to enhance their political influence inside Russia. NATO expansion eastward could be interpreted, for example, as a threat to Russian security. This is an especially salient consideration in the case of Russia, given Moscow's historic fear of encirclement by the more prosperous and technologically advanced states of Europe. As Jack Snyder (1989: 6) points out, perceptions of a deteriorating security environment can "decisively strengthen the hand of imperialists, militarists, and protectionists in the domestic politics of a weakly institutionalized liberal regime."

Such a development would, of course, have two unfortunate effects. First, it could jeopardize the process of political and economic liberalization within Russia. Second, it could prompt Russian foreign policy makers to adopt a less cooperative, and perhaps even a more confrontational, approach toward the United States and other countries. Obviously, this outcome would seriously complicate the pursuit of the grand strategy of institutionalization in Europe as a whole.

In light of this, the United States has not looked favorably upon proposals that would expand NATO membership in the near future. The Clinton administration, for example, does support the principle of enlarging NATO, but only "at an appropriate time," which presumably will come only near the end of this decade (if then) (Christopher, 1993c: 23). Indeed, the Clinton administration has made it virtually impossible for Eastern European countries to join NATO anytime soon by establishing certain "domestic eligibility requirements" that states must meet before they can even be considered for admission. These criteria are part of a broader initiative that the Clinton administration calls "Partnership for Peace."

This policy was approved by President Clinton on October 19, 1993 (Lippman, 1993: A28). It was subsequently embraced by NATO during the January 1994 summit in Brussels (Drozdiak and Williams, 1994: A1). In essence, Partnership for Peace establishes a process whereby states can become candidates for admission into NATO. As explained by former Secretary of Defense Les Aspin (1993), the process basically consists of a lengthy probationary period followed by a formal review of a state's suitability for membership.

As it presently stands, the policy consists of NATO issuing an invitation to the twenty-two states comprising the NACC, "and other European states on which NATO can agree," to sign a declaration indicating their willingness to enter into a partnership with the alliance. According to

Aspin (1993: 2), "Each new partner would then identify the facilities, resources, and forces it is willing to make available to the Partnership, and the extent of its intention to participate in joint training, planning and operations."

The partnership also would establish a commitment to consult in the event of emergencies: "Allies and partners would agree to consult whenever the territorial integrity, political independence, or security of a partner state was threatened" (Aspin, 1993: 3). Partnership, however, would not entitle these states to protection under NATO's collective security provision. Aspin (1993: 3) made this point explicit by stating: "Article Five of the North Atlantic Treaty requires each member to regard an attack against one as an attack against all. The Article Five guarantee would not be extended to partners." Nor would partnership automatically entitle states to membership in NATO:

> Partners for Peace would not automatically become eligible for membership in NATO. . . . On the other hand, Partners for Peace would have an opportunity to work with NATO to develop the principles, purposes and capabilities of NATO members. While partnership is no guarantee of membership, active participation would likely be an essential condition of future NATO membership. (Aspin, 1993: 3)

Ultimately, a state's eligibility for membership will be judged on the basis of its demonstrated commitment to democracy, capitalism, and an active record of participation in NATO's military endeavors (Aspin, 1993: 4). As this statement suggests, the decision to enlarge NATO will not be made solely on the basis of external threats. To qualify for membership, states must be characterized, internally, by liberal values and institutions. Given the unprecedented challenges confronting the process of political and economic reform in the countries of Eastern Europe and the former Soviet Union, this domestic eligibility requirement would seem to have the practical effect of rendering the question of NATO membership moot for the foreseeable future.

Over the last five years, U.S. foreign policy makers have supported initiatives that would serve to enhance NATO's political role in Europe. This has led to a series of institutional innovations designed to establish new patterns of political association between the alliance and its former adversaries in the East. The North Atlantic Cooperation Council and the Clinton administration's Partnership for Peace initiative constitute the most noteworthy achievements to date.

The United Nations

The United Nations is a general purpose international organization presently comprised of 185 members. Established on June 26, 1945, the

UN was created primarily in the name of maintaining international peace and security (Bennett, 1991: 53). This is reflected, for example, in Article 1(1) of the Charter, which states that the purposes of the United Nations are:

> To maintain international peace and security, and to that end: to take effective collective measures for the prevention and removal of threats to the peace, and for the suppression of acts of aggression or other breaches of the peace, and to bring about by peaceful means, and in conformity with the principles of justice and international law, adjustment or settlement of international disputes or situations which lead to a breach of the peace.

To this end, the Charter establishes: (1) a Security Council, which is to exercise "primary responsibility for the maintenance of international peace and security" (Article 24[1]); (2) procedures relating to the peaceful settlement of disputes (Chapter VI); and (3) an array of sanctions that can be invoked in response to a "threat to the peace" (Chapter VII).

The Security Council stands as the United Nations' key decisionmaking forum in regard to international security issues. Article 39 grants the Security Council the authority to "determine the existence of any threat to the peace" and to "decide what measures shall be taken" in response. Moreover, UN members are legally obligated to comply unconditionally with any and all Security Council decisions. This unprecedented commitment is contained in Article 25: "The Members of the United Nations agree to accept and carry out the decisions of the Security Council in accordance with the present Charter."

The Security Council itself consists of five permanent members (the United States, Russia, Britain, France, and China) and ten nonpermanent members who serve two-year terms. Each permanent member also possesses a veto that can be exercised in regard to all substantive questions (Article 27[3]). To approve resolutions relating to such issues, the Security Council requires an affirmative vote of nine members as well as the concurring votes of each permanent member.

Throughout most of its history, the United Nations has played a rather limited role in the realm of international security management. This can be attributed primarily to the Cold War, which inhibited the permanent members of the Security Council from engaging in the far-reaching collaborative acts envisioned in the Charter. As a result, UN security-related activities have been confined largely to the realm of mediation and peacekeeping operations (Durch, 1993). While these measures certainly are not unimportant to the maintenance of international peace and security, they are a far cry from the mandate established by the architects of this institution (Claude, 1959: 250–294).

Since the end of the Cold War, however, scholars and policymakers alike have expressed renewed interest in the United Nations as a tool for the management of international security issues. This is true of U.S. foreign policy makers as well, especially under the Clinton administration. To this end, the United States recently has advocated a series of institutional innovations that would serve to strengthen the United Nations' capacities in the realm of security.

To date, few of these proposals have been acted upon by the UN; fewer still have been implemented. Even so, a brief examination of these recommendations is warranted. U.S. foreign policy makers have come to regard the United Nations as a "necessary complement" to regionally based security institutions in Europe and elsewhere (Bush, 1992b: 60; Clinton, 1993c: 51). Perhaps more important, these initiatives also clearly reveal the extent to which collective security has emerged as one of the basic organizing concepts of the United States' approach to the post–Cold War era. Hence, a brief discussion of these proposals will shed additional light on the United States' efforts to address the security-related aspects of the grand strategy of institutionalization.

U.S. interest in the United Nations was sparked by the UN's performance in regard to Iraq's invasion of Kuwait. In the eyes of U.S. foreign policy makers, this experience demonstrated that the permanent members of the Security Council were capable of cooperating within the context of a major international crisis; it also indicated that the UN could serve as an effective tool for mobilizing and coordinating a collective response to a serious security problem (Bush 1991a, 1991b, 1992b; Clinton 1992a, 1992b, 1993d). In essence, the UN's success in the Gulf War raised the possibility of establishing a viable system of collective security in the post–Cold War era.

This theme was implicit in George Bush's vision of a "New World Order" in which "solidarity against aggression," orchestrated through the United Nations, would become a constitutive principle of international relations (*AFP*, 1990: 18–19; Bush, 1991b: 72; 1992b: 59). The president elaborated on this point during an April 1991 address at Maxwell Air Force Base in Montgomery, Alabama.

> The new world order . . . refers to new ways of working with other nations to deter aggression and achieve stability, to achieve prosperity, and, above all, to achieve peace. This order . . . got its first real test in the Gulf war. . . . By joining forces to defend one small nation, we showed that we can work together against aggressors in defense of principles. We must build on the successes of Desert Storm to give shape and momentum to this new world order. (Bush, 1991a: 32–33)

The Clinton administration has continued to emphasize this theme. When running for the presidency, for example, Bill Clinton (1992a: 11) pledged to build on the "Desert Storm experience" as part of a more broadly based effort "to reinvent the institutions of collective security." This commitment was reaffirmed by Warren Christopher during his confirmation hearings before the Senate Foreign Relations Committee. In his opening statement to the committee, the secretary of state designate announced that "it will be our administration's policy to encourage other nations and the institutions of collective security, especially the United Nations, to do more of the world's work to deter aggression, relieve suffering, and keep the peace" (Christopher, 1993e: 10).

Since taking office, however, Madeline Albright has emerged as the Clinton administration's chief spokesperson in regard to the United Nations and the principle of collective security. In a major speech delivered to the Foreign Policy Association in New York, Albright framed the United Nations as being "at the center of a new paradigm" in international politics: an emerging order in which "much, if not all, of the work needed to restore . . . failed states, to reform . . . defiant regimes, and to receive . . . new democracies falls into our lap at the United Nations" (Albright, 1993b: 30).

Albright's comment is instructive because it also provides an indication of the wide range of tasks that the Clinton administration associates with the concept of collective security. Whereas, traditionally, the jurisdictional scope of a collective security system has been limited to defending states in the event of external attack, the Clinton administration's conception encompasses a number of activities that go beyond merely deterrence and defense. Albright emphasized this point during an appearance before a joint session of the House and Senate Subcommittees on Europe, International Security, and International Organization in May 1993.

> If there is one overall theme that I want to stress today, it is that collective security has broadened in theory and practice to encompass far more than military remedies to keep the peace. . . . Another dimension of collective security today is state-building operations. . . . The role of a modern collective security system in facilitating democracy has been and will continue to be essential. . . . A further dimension of collective security is its vital role in protecting human rights, particularly the rights of ethnic minorities and other groups. (Albright, 1993c: 66–67)

To transform the UN into the centerpiece of a viable system of collective security, U.S. foreign policy makers have promoted a series of initiatives that would "strengthen the United Nations' ability to prevent, contain, and resolve conflict across the globe" (Bush, 1992b: 60). Most of these recommendations have centered on the United Nations' peacekeeping capabilities. During his farewell address to the General Assembly, for example, President Bush (1992b: 60) called upon member states to provide

the United Nations with the men, money, material, and organizational resources necessary for international peacekeeping missions. For the United
States' part, Bush pledged that it would move immediately to: (1) establish
"a permanent peacekeeping curriculum in U.S. military schools," (2) make
U.S. bases and facilities available for multinational peacekeeping training
and field exercises, and (3) increase U.S. "support for monitoring, verifi-
cation, reconnaissance, and other requirements of UN peacekeeping operations" (Bush, 1992b: 60).

The Clinton administration has continued to work toward the establishment of a "more efficient and regularized system of peacekeeping" in
the United Nations (Albright, 1993b: 32). This commitment is reflected,
for example, in Presidential Decision Directive 13 (PDD-13), which was
signed by President Clinton on July 14, 1993. The directive indicates that
the United States will endeavor to strengthen the United Nations' peacekeeping capabilities by: (1) doubling the size of the UN's peacekeeping
headquarters staff; (2) establishing a military intelligence division; (3) establishing an operations division featuring encrypted command, control,
and communications capabilities; (4) creating a rapidly deployable peacekeeping headquarters team; and (5) providing the United Nations with a
standing airlift capability to facilitate the rapid deployment of peacekeeping forces (Gellman, 1993a: A1).

PDD-13 also revealed that the Clinton administration was willing to
place U.S. military forces under the "operational control" of UN commanders and that it would provide an inventory of the capabilities and materiel
that the United States would be willing to make available to the United
Nations in support of peacekeeping missions (Gellman, 1993a: A1). The
document does not, however, establish a freestanding commitment to provide any specific military units to the United Nations.[15]

In addition to these measures, the Clinton administration has promoted
a number of other initiatives to strengthen the United Nations (Albright,
1993b: 30–33). Of these, the most politically significant recommendation
concerns the United States' support for adding Germany and Japan to the
Security Council as permanent members (Clinton, 1992a: 12; Albright,
1993b: 32). This would establish an institutionalized forum wherein all of
the major powers of Europe (and Eurasia) would stand as relative equals.
This is a potentially important innovation given the Clinton administration's evident desire to push the UN's military activities beyond the realm
of traditional peacekeeping. As permanent members, Germany and Japan
also would be expected to assume a more active role in global peace and
security efforts. This, in turn, could translate into greater German and
Japanese contributions in regard to the manpower, material, and financial
costs of UN operations (Clinton, 1992a: 12). I will return to this issue in
Chapter 5.

Conclusion

Over the past five years, U.S. foreign policy makers have attempted to deal with the security vacuum resulting from the collapse of the Cold War order by constructing a new architecture for European security. The United States' efforts have consisted primarily of: (1) a series of arms control initiatives designed to diminish the level of militarization on the Continent and to heighten the degree of military transparency between and among states; (2) an ongoing effort to develop a "strategic partnership" with Russia; and (3) a variety of proposals that would serve to broaden and deepen the role international institutions play in the management of regional security affairs. In the next chapter, I examine the problems and possibilities associated with the United States' attempt to create a viable system of collective security in post–Cold War Europe.

Notes

1. Germany stands as an exception to this statement. German troop strength was subject to negotiation within the context of the so-called Two-plus-Four talks. A ceiling on the size of German military forces is specified in the Treaty on the Final Settlement with Respect to Germany. The text of the agreement can be found in *Foreign Policy Bulletin* (November/December 1990) 1:2–4.

2. The aircraft are configured to carry both gravity bombs and nuclear-tipped cruise missiles (IISS, 1992: 235).

3. A fact sheet released by the White House regarding the treaty can be found in *Foreign Policy Bulletin* (May/June 1992) 2:38–39.

4. The text of the agreement can be found in *AFP* (1990: 289–292).

5. The text of the declaration can be found in *Foreign Policy Bulletin* (July/August 1992) 3:12–14.

6. The Vancouver Declaration was signed on April 4, 1993, by Presidents Clinton and Yeltsin at the conclusion of their first summit meeting. The text can be found in *Foreign Policy Bulletin* (May/June 1993) 3:27–28.

7. The text of this document can be found in *Foreign Policy Bulletin* (January/April 1992) 2:74–76.

8. The text of the Final Act can be found in *Foreign Policy Bulletin* (September/October 1992) 3:58–61.

9. Baker was quick to point out, however, that CSCE faced some inherent limitations when it came to the task of international conflict management in the region.

> These provisions give CSCE, for the first time, an orderly set of procedures to prevent and manage conflicts. In the end, of course, the resolution of problems within the Euro-Atlantic community will depend upon the willingness of countries to use the instruments which the CSCE has devised and the commitment of countries to live by the principles for which CSCE stands. (Baker, 1992a: 63)

10. In addition to this functional role, U.S. foreign policy makers also have emphasized NATO's symbolic significance in the Continent. Seen from this perspective, NATO stands as an exemplar of a distinctively liberal form of political

association and state sociality in the realm of security: to wit, a pluralistic security community that sets an important example for the countries of Eastern Europe. Baker stressed this point in his seminal address before the Berlin Press Club on December 12, 1989.

> NATO may have its greatest and most lasting effect on the pattern of change by demonstrating to the nations of the East a fundamentally different approach to security. NATO's four decades offer a vision of cooperation, not coercion; of open borders, not iron curtains. The reconciliation of ancient enemies, which has taken place under the umbrella of NATO's collective security, offers the nations of Eastern Europe an appealing model of international relations. (*AFP,* 1989: 301–302)

11. The text of the declaration can be found in *AFP* (1990: 275–278).

12. The text of the Rome Declaration can be found in *Foreign Policy Bulletin* (January/April 1992) 2:55–59.

13. Eagleburger succeeded James Baker as secretary of state in August 1992.

14. The Communique of the Ministerial Meeting of the North Atlantic Council can be found in *Foreign Policy Bulletin* (July/August 1992) 3:61–63.

15. In its original form, PDD-13 also authorized U.S. military personnel to disobey UN orders considered to be illegal, outside the UN mandate, or militarily unsound (Gellman, 1993a: A1). This provision provoked criticism from both the Secretary-General of the United Nations and the UN's Undersecretary for Peacekeeping on the grounds that it constituted a veto that would render authoritative UN command impossible. The Clinton administration responded to this by eliminating the provision from a subsequent draft of PDD-13 (Gellman, 1993b: A32).

3

EUROPE'S NASCENT
COLLECTIVE SECURITY SYSTEM

Multilateral security institutions play a prominent role in the United States' grand strategy of institutionalization. In essence, U.S. foreign policy makers look to CSCE, NATO, and the UN to fill the security vacuum created by the collapse of the Cold War order in Europe. This multi-institutional design is to serve as the principal mechanism for managing the domestic and international conflicts that may arise during Europe's transition to a liberal international society.

Conceptually, Europe's emerging security architecture constitutes a nascent collective security system. It is based upon the principle that security is indivisible among the countries comprising the European states system. It also is premised on the belief that regional peace and stability can best be maintained through the multilateral management of international security issues. It is the freestanding and unconditional commitments contained in the North Atlantic Treaty and the United Nations Charter, however, that most closely resemble the key characteristic of a collective security system. In principle, both documents commit the respective members of these institutions to respond to any and all acts of aggression.

In principle, a collective security system is well suited to carry out the order-keeping tasks envisioned by U.S. foreign policy makers. Such a system, for example, would establish a robust deterrent to aggression that should dramatically lower the likelihood of conflict in Europe. In practice, however, this form of international organization is characterized by obstacles to cooperation that can limit its effectiveness as a tool for the management of international security issues. To wit, a collective security system creates strong incentives for states to free ride on the efforts of other members. This problem, in turn, can jeopardize not only the effectiveness of the institution, but its durability as well.

Many analysts contend, however, that contemporary conditions in Europe should enable CSCE, NATO, and the UN to overcome the collective action problems that have undermined multilateral approaches in the past.

Of the factors cited in support of this claim, none is more important than the fact that all of the major powers of Europe currently are led by democratically oriented governments. This is an unprecedented political development that presumably will serve to encourage and sustain major-power security cooperation in the post–Cold War era.

This prospect is of enormous importance to the future of Europe's nascent collective security system because multilateral institutions depend heavily upon a minilateralist core of major-power cooperation (Kahler, 1992: 707; Morgan, 1993: 352). In practice, a collective security system is unlikely to be politically viable unless the major powers are willing to collaborate in the realm of security; hence, the presumed importance of the major powers' embrace of democratic values and institutions. In essence, the conventional wisdom holds that democratization has established a domestic political foundation conducive to the multilateral management of European security affairs.

The purpose of this chapter is twofold. The first is to examine the relative strengths and weaknesses of a collective security system. This portion of the analysis will highlight the many advantages associated with this type of international security institution; it also will discuss the free rider problem that is inherent in all systems of collective security. The second purpose of the chapter is to examine the factors deemed necessary to the establishment of a viable system of collective security. As part of this discussion, I will elaborate upon the theoretical linkage that presumably exists between democratization and major-power cooperation in the realm of security.

The Nature of Collective Security Systems

A collective security system can best be characterized as an international regime designed to limit the frequency and severity of international conflict through a multilateral commitment to oppose any and all acts of aggression.[1] In this section, I examine the internal architecture of a collective security system and identify the normative and instrumental dimensions of this distinctive type of international security institution. I begin with a brief discussion of international regimes and the role they play in international politics.

An international regime can be defined as "principles, norms, rules, and decision-making procedures around which actor expectations converge in a given issue-area" (Krasner, 1983: 1).[2] Its purpose is to mediate the collective action problems that can arise whenever states must coordinate their policy choices in order to arrive at a mutually desirable outcome (Stein, 1983: 120–127; Keohane 1989: 5–7; 1984: 85–88; Young, 1989:

5–6).[3] A regime performs this function by specifying principles, norms, and rules that serve as guidelines for making decisions under conditions of strategic interdependence (Stein, 1983: 132). Scholars are drawn to the study of international regimes by an underlying presumption that variations in the institutionalization of international politics can make a significant difference in terms of both state practices and systemic outcomes (Keohane, 1989: 2). This expectation is based upon two considerations.

First, international regimes shape the way states relate to, and interact with, one another (Krasner, 1983: 1–5; Young, 1989: 32; Keohane, 1989: 33). Put differently, the principles, norms, and rules associated with a regime specify the "actions that members are expected to perform (or to refrain from performing) under appropriate circumstances" (Young, 1989: 16). In theory, these practices can range from extremely competitive and conflictual behaviors to highly cooperative and pacific patterns of association (Wendt, 1992; Caporaso, 1992).[4] Hence, the substantive content of a regime can affect the nature of state sociality and, by implication, the prospects for peace and stability in the international system.

Second, international regimes also may influence the way states and societies develop over time. In joining a regime, a government may have to develop or acquire certain types of capabilities and/or skills in order to engage in the practices associated with the institution. Hence, participating in a regime can lead states and societies to develop certain material attributes, forms of expertise, and perhaps conceptions of self-interest that otherwise might not have emerged (Ashley, 1980: 10–50; 1984: 273–279). As a consequence, international regimes may play a constitutive role in the historical development of both states and societies (Keohane, 1989: 6; Dessler, 1989: 454–458; Wendt, 1992). Put differently, membership in an institution may shape not only the behavior of a state, but its identity as well.

This presumption, of course, stands at the core of the United States' grand strategy of institutionalization. To help nurture the development of liberal values and institutions in the countries of Eastern Europe and the former Soviet Union, U.S. foreign policy makers are striving to embed these states in a web of international economic and security regimes (e.g., CSCE, NACC, IMF [International Monetary Fund], GATT [General Agreement on Tariffs and Trade], and the World Bank). In theory, this should serve to reinforce the process of liberalization within these countries by socializing them to liberal norms and procedures in both issue-areas.

The regulatory and constitutive effects that international regimes exert in international politics help to account for the allure of a collective security system. If the institution can be established, it promises to deliver a relatively high degree of security at a greatly reduced level of militarization. This should serve to enhance state sociality by diminishing the degree of anxiety, suspicion, and rivalry that governments experience in regard to one another. It also should support the process of domestic liberalization by obviating the need for each state to maintain a large peacetime military establishment. In essence, collective security can promote the democratization and marketization of state-society relations by eliminating the security justifications for highly centralized governments and the extractive demands they place on their respective societies.

Before turning to a more systematic consideration of the benefits associated with a collective security system, however, I need to specify the principles, norms, rules, and decisionmaking procedures that characterize the regime. This will establish a basic conceptual framework that then can be used to assess the relative strengths and weaknesses of the system. The remainder of this section is devoted to a discussion of this issue.

A collective security system is based, first and foremost, on the principle that peace and security are indivisible among states. Hence, an act of aggression committed against one state is regarded as a latent threat to the security of all states (Ruggie, 1992: 571). This conceptualization, of course, suggests that the security of states is tightly coupled and highly interdependent. In this sense, a collective security system echoes the beliefs associated with the so-called domino theory (see Jervis and Snyder, 1991). Both perspectives agree that the fate of a single country can hold important implications for the other members of the international system. As a consequence, no act of aggression can be ignored or allowed to stand. To do so would simply invite further acts of aggression.

Collective security systems also are premised on the notion that all states should participate in the management of international security problems. This norm follows naturally from the strategic interdependence that characterizes state relations in the realm of security. Since an act of aggression constitutes a latent threat to the security of everyone, all states are expected to contribute to activities related to the maintenance of international peace and stability.

The norm also is a consequence of the fact that "sovereign equality" stands as one of the basic ordering principles of a collective security system. Organizationally, the principle extends to each member of the regime equal rights and responsibilities when it comes to the making and implementation of decisions. Sovereign equality is justified, both philosophically and legally, on the basis of sovereignty and the juridical equality this principle establishes among the members of the interstate system (Klein, 1974; Jackson, 1990). Hence, in a collective security system, all states are expected to contribute to efforts to manage international security problems.

This norm is codified in the form of a rule that members of the institution are expected to adhere to unconditionally: Each state is committed to respond to any and all acts of aggression (Thompson, 1953; Wolfers, 1962: 181–204). This constitutes an automatic and legally binding obligation that members must honor whenever and wherever aggression occurs. The logic underlying the rule, of course, is that a freestanding multilateral commitment to oppose aggression will serve to both deter and reassure states.

> The expectation of collective resistance to aggression is conceived as a deterrence threat to states which might be tempted to misuse their power and a promise of security to all states which might be subject to attack. The scheme is collective in the fullest sense; it purports to provide security for *all* states, *by* the actions of all states, *against* all states which might challenge the existing order by the arbitrary unleashing of their power. (Claude, 1962: 110)

Indivisibility and the multilateral acceptance of an unconditional obligation to abide by a generalized rule of behavior: These are the essential properties of a collective security system. CSCE, NATO, and the UN all embody these characteristics. As noted previously, Article 5 of the North Atlantic Treaty explicitly commits the signatories to respond to any and all acts of external aggression perpetrated against any of its members. Similarly, Article 1 of the UN Charter commits states "to take effective collective measures for the prevention and removal of threats to the peace, and for the suppression of acts of aggression or other breaches of the peace." While CSCE does not involve such a commitment per se, the Charter of Paris does obligate states to abide "unreservedly" by the "Ten Principles" of international relations contained in the Helsinki summit's Final Act (CSCE, November 21, 1990: 76).

Obviously, a collective security system is a very demanding form of international association. In practice, it requires states to forgo "the temptation to define their interests narrowly in terms of national interests" (Caporaso, 1993: 56) and to manifest a form of empathy: a concern for the welfare of other states even when their fate does not seem to have any direct bearing on the security or well-being of one's own state (Keohane, 1984: 123). Put differently, membership in a collective security system obligates a state to get involved in international conflicts regardless of whether or not the crisis has direct and immediate implications for its own security.

Hence, by joining this type of institution, states dramatically expand the scope of their security concerns and responsibilities. This raises the obvious question of why states would want to participate in such a system. The answer to this lies in the considerable benefits a collective security system can confer on its members.

The Benefits of Collective Security

There are three principal benefits that a collective security system can deliver. First, it should dramatically lower the frequency of international conflict. Second, the regime also should promote international cooperation. Third, a collective security will establish a benign systemic environment that should facilitate the spread and consolidation of liberal values and institutions at the level of domestic politics. In this section, I elaborate on each of these points.

A collective security system should diminish the frequency of international conflict because the multilateral security guarantee associated with the regime should serve as a highly robust deterrent to aggression (Claude, 1962: 111). There are two basic reasons for this. First, the existence of a legally binding, and internationally recognized, security commitment increases the likelihood that states will intervene in a conflict involving another member of the institution (Siverson and King, 1979).[5] This, in turn, should diminish a would-be aggressor's uncertainty about whether or not the initiation of conflict would draw a response from other members of the international community (Kupchan and Kupchan, 1991: 125). By reducing uncertainty, a collective security system also should decrease the probability of wars resulting from miscalculation (Levy, 1989: 234).

Second, this type of regime also confronts a would-be aggressor with the prospect of being opposed by a broadly based international coalition possessing preponderant military capabilities (Claude, 1962: 111). Under these circumstances, the resort to force should be unprofitable since a single state could never mobilize sufficient forces to defeat the coalition.[6] By dramatically lowering the expected utility of war, collective security systems thereby neutralize a factor that previous research has established as a necessary condition for the initiation of international conflict (Bueno de Mesquita, 1981).

A second benefit associated with a collective security system is that it should promote international cooperation since the regime ameliorates many of the risks states face when participating in a collaborative undertaking. Theorists have identified two major factors that can inhibit international security cooperation: relative gains considerations and the fear of cheating (Grieco, 1988).[7] The concept of relative gains refers to the way the benefits of cooperation are distributed between and among participants (Waltz, 1979: 105; Grieco, 1988: 499). Ideally, one would hope that benefits are distributed equitably.[8] Yet, in practice, governments must consider the possibility that one state may benefit more than another. This, in turn, can create security concerns about the future that block cooperation in the present.

States fear that their partners will achieve relatively greater gains; that, as a result, the partners will surge ahead of them in relative capabilities; and, finally, that their increasingly powerful partners in the present could become all the more formidable foes at some point in the future. (Grieco, 1988: 499)[9]

Such concerns, of course, are exacerbated by the difficulties governments face when it comes to forecasting in international politics. The interstate system is characterized by a set of complex interconnections and linkages that obscures basic cause-and-effect relationships in international politics (Jervis, 1991–1992: 40–42). It is thus difficult for states to estimate what consequences a policy initiative will have as it ramifies throughout the system. Typically, the best a government can do is arrive at a probabilistic forecast of what is likely to occur under a given set of conditions (Gaddis, 1992–1993). Unfortunately, tightly coupled systems also are prone to shocks and revolutionary developments that can quickly lead to quite unexpected outcomes (Perrow, 1984). Such structural uncertainty can render governments wary of cooperative undertakings, especially in the realm of security where even "small errors can have big consequences" (Jervis, 1978: 175).

The intangible nature of security itself poses an additional problem in this regard. Security is primarily a subjective phenomenon that lacks clearly defined empirical referents (Wolfers, 1962: 150). This makes it very difficult to measure the amount of security a country presently has or how much it may have in the future (Jervis, 1983: 175). This, in turn, severely complicates the analytical task of estimating what the relative gains from international security cooperation actually will be, how the benefits will be distributed, and how the distribution may affect a state's national security over time.

A similar set of concerns prompts decisionmakers to worry about the problem of cheating.[10] This can pose a threat to state security if "one player, by defecting, can reap rewards [that place] the other player at an immediate and overwhelming disadvantage" (Lipson, 1984: 14). In practice, there are two dimensions to the problem. First, decisionmakers must try to estimate what consequences are likely to follow if another state does in fact cheat. Will defection provide "immediate and overwhelming" advantages, or will it lead to only marginal benefits accruing over a longer period of time? Here again, the uncertainties associated with forecasting in international politics can lead decisionmakers to exaggerate the potentially harmful effects of defection.[11]

Second, governments must determine whether their surveillance and monitoring capabilities will enable them to detect defections in a timely fashion. Early warning monitors can diminish some of the risks associated with cheating by providing governments with an opportunity to detect and react to defections before they can become really damaging (Stein, 1985: 615; Lipson, 1984: 16). Unfortunately, turbidity is the rule rather than the exception in international politics when it comes to assessing the intentions and behavior of states (Snyder and Jervis, 1992).[12]

A collective security system, however, should mediate states' concerns about relative gains and cheating. It does so by establishing a reassuring environment that dramatically lowers the risk of being exploited. Relative gains considerations, for example, should be muted within this type of system because state security is no longer premised solely upon self-help capabilities. The security guarantees associated with the institution should render states much less sensitive to relative gains considerations because even a highly asymmetrical distribution of benefits would not enhance the expected utility of conflict from the perspective of a would-be aggressor. Similarly, the problem of cheating also would become much less important within the context of a collective security system. Even persistent violations of an agreement would not seriously jeopardize the security of states because the multilateral security commitment provides governments with such a wide margin of surplus security.

A collective security system also should facilitate cooperation by promoting a relatively benign form of state sociality. In this type of system, states will regard one another with much less anxiety, suspicion, and rivalry because governments no longer have to depend solely upon self-help measures to defend their political autonomy and territorial integrity. In this sense, the regime constitutes a form of insurance that will enable states to take a more relaxed attitude toward the other members of the international community. By nurturing a more pacific pattern of international association, a collective security system can foster a sense of trust and confidence on the part of states that should encourage them to engage in collaborative acts that would be unthinkable in a more highly competitive environment (Kupchan and Kupchan, 1991: 134).

Along the same lines, a collective security system also should enhance the prospects for international cooperation by providing states with an organizational setting that can facilitate international bargaining. This type of regime will necessitate the creation of a standing international organization since states will need a fixed base of operations and a permanent bureaucracy in order to manage the logistics associated with the mobilization and coordination of the members' response to an act of aggression (see Young, 1989: 46–47). In principle, this organizational setting can be conducive to international cooperation in other issue-areas as well. An international organization can serve this purpose by: (1) routinizing consultative and communicative procedures; (2) disseminating information to its members; (3) providing state representatives with a ready-made forum for exchanging views, identifying common interests, and formulating mutually accepted arrangements; and (4) creating opportunities for establishing cross-issue linkages (Keohane, 1984: 100–103; Kupchan and Kupchan, 1991: 130–133; Martin, 1992). In essence, a collective security system can enhance the prospects for international cooperation by institutionalizing transparency and habits of cooperation.

A third potential benefit of collective security stems from the constitutive effects the regime may exert on the internal characteristics of states and societies. In principle, a collective security system should facilitate the spread of liberal values and institutions at the level of domestic politics because it weakens the justification for highly centralized forms of governments and the extractive demands they place on society. Conceptually, the argument is based upon Otto Hintze's well-known contention: "The form and spirit of the state's organization will not be determined solely by economic and social forces and clashes of interests, but primarily by the necessities of defense and offense" (Hintze, quoted in Deudney and Ikenberry, 1991–1992: 82).[13]

A collective security system could affect the historical development of states and societies principally by diminishing the need for states to maintain large peacetime military establishments. In the absence of a collective security system, states will engage in balance-of-power practices (Claude, 1962: 93). This can inhibit the development of liberal values and institutions within a country because a highly competitive systemic environment can promote the growth and consolidation of a state's power vis-à-vis society (Tilly, 1975).

In a balance-of-power system, states seek to ensure their security by acquiring military capabilities sufficient to deter, or defend against, aggression (Wolfers, 1962: 117–132). Historically, states have attempted to achieve this strategic objective through a combination of alliance formation and the internal mobilization of their own societal resources (Waltz, 1979: 118). The latter approach, of course, can profoundly shape the internal development of a country because internal mobilization creates strong incentives for the state to expand its power relative to society.

To field and maintain its own military forces, a state needs to extract men, money, and material from society (Huntington, 1961). This encourages the state to increase its administrative capacity to monitor and penetrate society (Mastanduno, Lake, and Ikenberry, 1989: 463; Barnett, 1990: 538). This also can inhibit the development of liberal-capitalist states, however, because it tends to blur the boundary between the public and private spheres of economic wealth that lies at the heart of this political formation (Ruggie, 1983; Cox, 1987: 219–230).

Moreover, internal mobilization will encourage the state, and especially military organizations, to promote self-serving myths designed "to convince society to grant them the size, wealth, autonomy, and prestige that all bureaucracies seek" (Van Evera, 1990–1991: 18). As part of this, a government will be encouraged to exaggerate the threat posed by other states and to emphasize the need for specialized knowledge (or expertise) in order to deal with the situation (Van Evera, 1990–1991: 19–21). As Barry Posen (1984: 45–46) points out, by mystifying the subject of national security, a state can insulate itself from domestic criticism while simultaneously increasing its chances of getting society to acquiesce to its resource demands. Obviously, this does not enhance the prospects for nurturing liberal-democratic norms and institutions premised on the principles of openness and accountability.

A state's extractive demands, of course, are unavoidably linked to the nature of the international environment. The more threatening a country's security predicament appears to be, the greater the claims the state will make on society and the more likely it becomes that society will regard these demands as legitimate (Herbst, 1990: 119–122). A balance-of-power system tends to exacerbate security concerns because the social relations characterizing this system are defined largely in terms of anxiety, hostility, rivalry, and mistrust (Wendt, 1992). In this type of system, after all, states seek to ensure their security basically by adopting mutually threatening military postures.

A collective security system, on the other hand, will create a relatively benign international environment that, in turn, can affect the course of the domestic political struggle between state and society by eliminating the need for a high level of national military preparedness. As noted previously, the existence of an institutionalized commitment to oppose any and all acts of aggression increases the likelihood that a state will receive assistance in the event that it is attacked. Hence, it becomes less essential for states to field and maintain large peacetime military establishments.

By obviating this need, a collective security system will provide societies with a rationalization for limiting the power of government and the societal resources to which the state legitimately can lay claim. This should serve to promote the democratization and marketization of state-society relations since liberal values and institutions constitute the most effective and efficient means of restraining state power. In essence, democracy and the marketplace establish a boundary between the public and private spheres of wealth and power that systematically privilege society at the expense of the state (Ruggie, 1983; Cox, 1987: 219–230). While the presence of a collective security is neither a necessary nor a sufficient condition for the emergence of liberal-capitalist states, the existence of such a regime should increase the likelihood that such political formations will emerge.

As the discussion in this section indicates, a collective security system is well suited to carry out the tasks envisioned by U.S. foreign policy makers. In principle, the regime would serve to: (1) lower the probability of international conflict in Europe, (2) promote regional cooperation, and (3) support the process of liberalization in the countries of Eastern Europe and the former Soviet Union. In practice, however, collective security systems are characterized by formidable collective action problems that can seriously undermine their effectiveness. The next section takes up this issue.

Collective Security and the Free Rider Problem

A collective security system is predicated upon states sharing a common interest in preventing the outbreak of conflict (Betts, 1992: 17). This is a necessary condition for the formation of such a system since it underlies the willingness of states to make an explicit commitment to respond to any and all acts of aggression. Despite the existence of this common interest, however, the states participating in a collective security system will encounter collective action problems that raise serious questions about the durability and effectiveness of the institution. To wit, collective security systems create strong incentives for states to free ride on the efforts of other members.

This section examines the free rider problem that is inherent in all collective security systems. Two factors are principally responsible for this existential dilemma. First, collective security is fundamentally a nonexcludable good, which means, in practice, that free riders cannot easily be prevented from enjoying the benefits of the institution. Second, the large number of states belonging to a collective security organization makes it possible for a member to free ride without jeopardizing the achievement of the collective good. The ensuing discussion elaborates on these points and highlights the critical role that the major powers can play in terms of overcoming the free rider problem.

I begin by specifying two axioms that clarify the dilemma confronting all types of international organization, including collective security systems.

A1: States participate in international organizations in the name of achieving some goal, or satisfying some interest, that could not be accomplished unilaterally.

A2: "Though all of the members of the group . . . have a common interest in obtaining this collective benefit, they have no common interest in paying the cost of providing the collective good. Each would prefer that the others pay the entire cost" (Olson, 1965: 21).

The difficulties states encounter in regard to collaborative situations also can be illustrated in terms of the familiar two-person Prisoners'

Dilemma. As Figure 3.1 indicates, both actors' dominant strategy is to engage in uncooperative behavior, regardless of what the other player does. If both actors pursue this strategy, of course, it will lead to an equilibrium outcome (i.e., both free ride), which is suboptimal from the standpoint of both.

To arrive at the Pareto-optimal outcome, the actors must agree to abandon their dominant strategy and commit to a cooperative approach. This still may not be enough to resolve the problem, however. As Lisa Martin (1993: 96) points out, even after a cooperative solution has been arranged, collaborative situations create "strong temptations to defect . . . since defection results in immediate payoffs" delivered at the expense of others. It is for this reason that states faced with a collaborative problem must take pains to "specify strict patterns of behavior and insure that no one cheats" (Stein, 1983: 128).

The Prisoners' Dilemma highlights the mixed incentives states confront within the context of any collective security system. On the one hand, the participants have a clear interest in seeing that the collective goal (i.e., peace and stability) is achieved. On the other hand, however, each state also would like the other members of the organization to bear the costs of producing the good. In this way, a noncontributor stands to maximize the net benefits it receives from belonging to the institution. This temptation arises because organizations produce collective goods characterized by the property of nonexclusivity. Hence, "those who do not purchase or pay for any of the public or collective good cannot be excluded or kept from sharing in the consumption of the good" (Olson, 1965: 15). It is the nonexcludable nature of public goods that creates such strong incentives to free ride on the efforts of other states.

It is this tension between the common interest and individual preferences that renders collective security systems inherently problematic. The incentives to free ride will emerge most clearly, of course, when it comes to honoring the regime's commitment to respond to any and all acts of aggression. Such undertakings will entail tangible costs for member states in the form of men, money, and/or material.[14] Hence, by reneging on its commitment to participate in such operations, a state stands to increase its benefits relative to the other members of the organization. Under such circumstances, a free rider would continue to enjoy the benefits of being a member of a collective security system (i.e., aggression is opposed) while bearing few of the costs associated with the provision of the good.

All things being equal, the temptation to adopt this strategy will increase as the magnitude of the expected costs associated with a collective action increases. Moreover, there is relatively little that can be done to effectively sanction free riders in this situation. Noncontributors, of course, could be expelled from the organization, but this would be counterproductive

---

Figure 3.1   The Prisoners' Dilemma

	Actor B	
	Contribute	Free Ride
Actor A		
Contribute	3,3	1,4
Free Ride	4,1	2,2

Source: Derived from Stein (1983).
Note: 4 = best payoff; 1 = worst payoff.

---

from the standpoint of the other members of the regime. Collective security is an "inclusive public good" in the sense that its value increases as more states participate in the regime (Olson, 1965: 40). As membership in the system grows, the pacifying effects of the multilateral security guarantee will spread as well. Hence, the benefits to be derived from this inclusive good will increase as the jurisdictional scope of the collective security system expands.

Expelling free riders from the organization, however, would serve to contract the system's geographic scope. This could have the unintended consequence of increasing the degree of instability and conflict in the region. Since ostracized states would be deprived of the system's collective security guarantees, they could become inviting targets from the standpoint of a would-be aggressor. Thus, punishing free riders through expulsion could have the pernicious effect of increasing the potential for international conflict. Since the systemic costs associated with an act of aggression would almost certainly be greater than the institutional costs that result from free riding, states are unlikely to retaliate against noncontributors by expelling them from the organization. Short of expulsion, however, there is really no practical way of preventing states from enjoying the benefits that accrue from membership in a collective security system.[15]

The free rider problem is inherent in all forms of international organization. The severity of the problem, however, will tend to vary along with the size of the organization. *Certis paribus,* larger organizations will create stronger incentives to free ride than will associations featuring fewer members. As Mancur Olson explains, this phenomenon is a consequence of the fact that

> when the number of participants is large, the typical participant will
> know that his own efforts will probably not make much difference to the
> outcome, and that he will be affected . . . in much the same way no mat-
> ter how much or little effort he puts into [it]. . . . [Thus] the contribution
> that each participant will make toward achieving or improving these pub-
> lic goods will become smaller as the [group] becomes larger. (Olson,
> 1965: 53)

In large voluntary associations, individuals will be tempted to free
ride because doing so is unlikely to seriously jeopardize the organization's
ability to achieve the collective good. Collective security systems are especially prone to this type of problem, of course, because they strive for
universal membership. This ensures that a relatively large number of states
will become members of the institution. While universal membership enhances the value of the collective good, it also increases the incentives for
states to free ride.

Moreover, this problem tends to be exacerbated within the context of
a collective security system because relatively minor military powers com-
prise the bulk of the institution's membership. In general, these states do
not possess the military capabilities needed to make a significant contribution to the organization's success. In practice, this responsibility typically devolves to a relatively small subgroup of major military powers
whose active participation is essential to the implementation of the system's collective security guarantees. As a consequence, less powerful
members of the institution are faced with strong incentives to free ride because their defection is unlikely to significantly diminish the organization's effectiveness in responding to an act of aggression. As this point
suggests, collective security systems create unique opportunities for the
weak to exploit the strong in the realm of security (see Snidal, 1985).

The collective action problems associated with a collective security
system raise serious doubts about its effectiveness as a tool for the management of international security affairs. The risk, of course, is that if
enough members pursue a free riding strategy, the organization may become incapable of producing the collective good (Olson, 1965: 44). This
is the so-called tyranny of small decisions whereby rational behavior on
the part of each individual leads to a collectively irrational outcome
(Waltz, 1979: 108). This possibility, in turn, may jeopardize not only the
effectiveness of the institution, but its durability as well.

Since there is no guarantee that members will be able to overcome the
collective action problems noted above, a state must remain sensitive to
the risk that it may be abandoned if aggression does occur (Snyder, 1984:
466). This implies that, in practice, "self-help" may still have to be the
guiding axiom of prudential statecraft even within the context of a collective security system. Obviously, such a development would constitute a
quite serious erosion of confidence in the institution's ability to preserve

the political autonomy and territorial integrity of its members. Such doubts, in turn, could weaken the regime and perhaps even threaten its very survival.

International relations theorists argue that the "shadow of the future" has an important bearing on the willingness of states to cooperate (Oye, 1985: 13–14). If governments expect a regime to last, they presumably will be more likely to continue participating in an institution. If, on the other hand, states have serious doubts about the durability of a cooperative arrangement, they may become more likely to defect. *Certis paribus,* the free rider problem should serve to diminish states' confidence in a collective security system. This may encourage decisionmakers to discount the future and to focus instead on securing short-term benefits. To the extent that the members of the institution come to embrace this attitude, multilateral cooperation should become more difficult to achieve and sustain, thereby jeopardizing the durability of a collective security system.

This section has outlined the free rider problem inherent in all collective security systems. The discussion also has implied, however, that these problems may be overcome if the major powers are willing and able to collaborate in the realm of security. In practice, the viability of a collective security system depends heavily upon a minilateralist core of major-power cooperation (Morgan, 1993: 352). It is the major powers, after all, who provide the bulk of the military capabilities that supply the institution with its credibility as a deterrent to aggression. Conceptually, the major powers are to be regarded as a "privileged group" that is capable of providing the collective good even when the other members of the organization opt to free ride (Olson, 1965: 49–50).[16] Hence, major-power cooperation stands as a necessary, and perhaps a sufficient, condition for the effective functioning of a collective security system (Kupchan and Kupchan, 1991).

This point is of enormous importance to the future of Europe's nascent collective security system. Like all institutions of collective security, CSCE, NATO, and the UN are all likely to be beset by the free rider problem. This also suggests that their effectiveness as a tool for the management of regional security affairs ultimately will hinge upon the major powers' willingness to engage in far-reaching acts of security cooperation. In the eyes of many observers, this bodes well for the construction of a collective security system in post–Cold War Europe. This optimism stems from a belief held by a number of analysts that contemporary systemic and domestic conditions are highly favorable to cooperation on the part of the major powers. We turn now to a consideration of this argument.

Major-Power Cooperation in Post–Cold War Europe

Historically, major powers have been reluctant to cooperate in the realm of security for the reasons outlined above. This, in part, helps to explain why collective security systems rarely are established in international politics. Indeed, the major powers have expressed an interest in constructing such a system on only three occasions over the past five centuries (Jervis, 1985: 58).

Many analysts contend, however, that recent revolutionary changes in the nature of international politics have created a unique opportunity to establish a viable system of collective security in Europe (Mueller, 1989a; Chalmers, 1990; Flynn and Scheffer, 1990; Goodby, 1991; Kupchan and Kupchan, 1991; Mueller, 1991; Rosecrance, 1992; Zelikow, 1992).[17] Of the factors cited in support of this claim, none is more important than the fact that all of the major powers of Europe currently are led by democratically oriented governments. This is an unprecedented political development that, theorists argue, should encourage the major powers to cooperate widely in the realm of security. In essence, the argument contends that democratization on the part of the major powers has established a domestic political foundation conducive to the multilateral management of European security issues.

In this section, I examine this hypothesis and the implications it holds for Europe's nascent collective security system. I begin with a brief discussion of the conditions that international relations theorists deem necessary for the formation of this type of multilateral institution.

Two cognitive factors are routinely cited as necessary conditions for the construction and maintenance of a collective security system (Jervis, 1983: 177–178; 1985: 64; Kupchan and Kupchan, 1991: 124–125, 146). First, decisionmakers must believe that war would lead to prohibitively high costs and, hence, must be avoided. Second, policymakers also must believe that unilateral measures will be inadequate to prevent the outbreak of international conflict. Only under conditions of mutual vulnerability and mutual dependence will the major powers express an interest in security cooperation (George, 1988: 644).

While necessary, these factors are far from sufficient to ensure the formation of a collective security system.[18] As noted previously, relative gains considerations can inhibit states from cooperating even when the prospective arrangement promises to benefit each of the participants. Similarly, concerns about cheating, combined with the problem of turbidity, can block cooperation by increasing a state's fear of being exploited in a collaborative situation. To overcome these obstacles, states must endeavor to reassure one another that: (1) they will honor the terms of the cooperative arrangement, and (2) they will not exploit the distribution of relative benefits in ways that would threaten the security of other states.

It is primarily in regard to the task of reassurance that democratization enhances the prospects for cooperation on the part of the major powers. In theory, there are two principal reasons why democracies inspire confidence and trust among one another. First, democracies are characterized by certain attributes that constrain governments from pursuing aggressive foreign policies (Snyder, 1991: 49–52). Hence, democratic states are prone to adopt defensive strategies that render them less threatening to other members of the international system. As Deudney and Ikenberry explain, there are four principal reasons for this.

> First, the structure of the liberal state itself impedes aggressive action because of its numerous constitutional checks on major war-making, and because its extensive system of deliberation and consultation tends to filter out rash and extreme ideas. Second, democracy empowers the broad mass of people, who have the most to lose from war, and therefore tend to hold their states back from war-making. Third, the capitalist system of private ownership of wealth provides a continuing check on the ability of the state apparatus to generate revenues for public purposes of all sorts, including war-making. Fourth, the pacific tenor of liberal democratic political culture and the non-martial character of consumer society further reduces the probability of liberal aggression, particularly against a well-armed state. (Deudney and Ikenberry, 1991–1992: 85–86)

Because democratic states are prone to adopt defensive strategies, democratization on the part of the major powers will tend to promote cooperation since it ameliorates the relative gains considerations that might otherwise prompt them to worry about the distributional consequences of their joint undertakings. This is reinforced by the fact that democracies rarely go to war with one another (Russett, 1993). Given the pacific nature of democratic dyads (Bremer, 1992), it is unlikely that an asymmetrical distribution of benefits will rebound to a state's disadvantage in the realm of security. This heightens the prospects for cooperation because it enables governments to adopt a longer-term perspective in which expectations of diffuse reciprocity prevail over short-term considerations.[19] In essence, democratization tends to lengthen the "shadow of the future" by increasing the probability that pacific and cooperative forms of international association will endure.

The second reason democracies inspire confidence and trust among one another is that they are characterized by a relatively high degree of openness that makes it easier for other governments to monitor their adherence to an international agreement (Cowhey, 1993: 302). Democracies facilitate transparency through their commitment to the free exchange of ideas, a free press, and open public debates (Van Evera, 1990–1991: 27). This promotes cooperation because openness can: (1) reassure states about the benign intentions of others, and (2) heighten the probability that a state will be able to detect uncooperative behavior before a damaging defection can occur. Hence, the transparency associated with democratization on the part of the major powers should encourage them to cooperate by diminishing the probability of, and the risks associated with, cheating.

In addition to these benefits, democratization also can enable the major powers to arrive at a normative consensus concerning the "essential features of a desirable international order" (Kupchan and Kupchan, 1991: 146). This can contribute to a shared sense of purpose that will encourage and sustain their cooperation. Kupchan and Kupchan (1991: 124) argue that political homogeneity is conducive to the formation of a collective security system because "the major powers of the day must have fundamentally compatible views of what constitutes a stable and acceptable international order."

Along the same lines, Flynn and Scheffer (1990: 83) contend that democratization will serve to establish a common commitment on the part of the major powers to "transfer to the international level . . . the domestic system of conflict resolution used by democracies." Indeed, these authors contend that democratization is a *necessary condition* for the creation of a collective security system.

> The relationship between collective security and democracy is as direct as that between concert and monarchy. . . . The members of any workable collective security system must be democracies. . . . Otherwise, the system will always risk falling prey to authoritarian regimes that reject the established rules of conflict resolution. (Flynn and Scheffer, 1990: 83)[20]

In sum, democratic major powers appear to be ideal candidates for membership because their openness and their preference for defensive strategies mute the security concerns that traditionally have complicated the task of international security cooperation. At the same time, however, their shared commitment to the promotion of liberal values and institutions constitutes a normative agenda that can serve to rally such countries around a common social purpose.

If this is the case, then contemporary conditions would appear to be highly favorable to the creation of a collective security system in post–Cold War Europe. Never before in the history of the European states system have so many of the major powers been characterized by liberal values and institutions at the level of their domestic political systems. The United States, Britain, France, and Germany, of course, are long-established and firmly rooted democracies; Russia can best be characterized as a "weakly institutionalized liberal regime" at present (Snyder, 1989: 6). This is an unprecedented political development that presumably has established a domestic foundation conducive to the multilateral management of European security affairs.

Conclusion

Over the centuries, scholars and policymakers have spent an enormous amount of time and energy trying to devise ways of limiting the frequency and severity of international conflict (Hinsley, 1963). Indeed, one is tempted to characterize this task as the most pressing public policy problem in the history of international politics (Osgood and Tucker, 1967: 3–40).

In theory, a collective security system would resolve this problem by establishing a multilateral security guarantee that would serve as a highly robust deterrent to aggression. This is a very demanding form of international association, however, that creates strong incentives for states to free ride on the efforts of others. These collective action problems, in turn, raise serious questions about both the effectiveness and the durability of the institution.

Many analysts contend, however, that a viable system of collective security can be established in post–Cold War Europe because democratization on the part of the major powers will encourage these states to engage in far-reaching acts of security cooperation. Hence, democratization will enable the major powers to act as a "privileged group" that can underwrite the institution's collective security guarantee regardless of whether or not the other members cooperate. Seen from this perspective, there are grounds for believing that the institutions comprising Europe's nascent collective security system will be able to serve as effective tools for the management of regional security affairs.

This argument, however, generally fails to consider how domestic politics can inhibit a state from participating in a collective security system. This is a serious omission given the important role that public opinion and other factors play in democracies. In the next chapter, I will address these issues as part of a broader discussion of why contemporary systemic and domestic conditions are not conducive to the functioning of a collective security system in post–Cold War Europe.

Notes

1. Historically, states have attempted to cope with the security problems posed by the anarchic structure of the international political system by engaging in balance-of-power practices. As a tool for the management of international security affairs, however, balance-of-power systems are characterized by a number of quite serious limitations. For a discussion of the institution and its many problems, see Claude (1962: 40–87).

2. Conceptually, there are two basic types of international institutions: conventions and regimes (Keohane, 1989: 4; Young, 1989: 13). A convention represents an "informal institution, with implicit rules and understandings, that shape the expectations of actors" (Keohane, 1989: 4). A regime, on the other hand, is an institution "with explicit rules, agreed upon by governments, that pertain to particular sets of issues in international politics" (Keohane, 1989: 4).

3. Collective action problems, of course, are pervasive in the realm of security. This can be attributed to the fact that security is a relational phenomenon that

inevitably involves some degree of strategic interdependence between and among states (Buzan, 1991: 187). This point has long been recognized by international relations theorists. The concept of the security dilemma, for example, neatly illustrates the point (Herz, 1950; Jervis, 1978).

4. The social relations characterizing a balance-of-power system, for example, tend to be defined largely in terms of anxiety, hostility, and mistrust (Wendt, 1992). The significance of this point is discussed below.

5. Siverson and King examined the effect that alliance ties had upon the diffusion of conflict among states during the nineteenth and twentieth centuries. The analysis revealed that states exhibit a greater tendency to intervene in conflicts when an ally is involved in a dispute. This contagion effect suggests that the states belonging to a collective security system should manifest a similar propensity to come to the assistance of a member who has been attacked. A collective security institution is, after all, an alliance writ large.

6. The advent of nuclear weapons would seem to undermine the strength of this deterrent. However, two advocates of collective security argue that nuclearization actually will strengthen the regime.

> Deterrence under collective security in a nuclear world would operate more strongly . . . [because] an aggressor would face an opposing coalition not only of preponderant conventional force but also of preponderant nuclear capability. (Kupchan and Kupchan, 1991: 127)

7. Domestic politics also can complicate the task of international cooperation (see Putnam, 1988; Evans, Jacobson, and Putnam, 1993). This point will be discussed in the following chapter.

8. An equitable distribution of benefits should not be confused with a symmetrical (or equal) distribution. The latter may not be acceptable if the participants are not starting from the same position.

9. Grieco (1988: 501) argues that a state's sensitivity to relative gains issues will be greatest when a government finds itself in circumstances "approximating a state of war." Specifically, Grieco hypothesizes that state sensitivity will increase: if the prospective partner is a longtime adversary; if cooperation yields benefits that can easily enhance the influence and/or capabilities of the partner; if a state's own relative capabilities already are declining; and if the cooperative act involves issues relating to national security.

10. Putnam (1988: 438) draws an important distinction between "voluntary" and "involuntary" defection. In the former, a state defects from a cooperative arrangement because of the strategic incentives to cheat that are present in the structure of the external situation. Involuntary defection, on the other hand, results from domestic political constraints that prevent a government from honoring the terms of an agreement with which it would otherwise prefer to comply. My use of the term "cheating" corresponds to Putnam's concept of voluntary defection.

11. The risk, of course, is that decisionmakers will conclude that they are involved in a zero-sum game wherein each government is seeking to maximize the relative difference between its own position and the positions held by others. When pure power motivations prevail, the potential for cooperation will diminish quite dramatically since relative gains considerations will then come to the fore (Krasner, 1983: 8). This conclusion follows because "the possibility of mutual benefit evaporates . . . when competitors play games of 'status' or 'difference'" (Stein, 1985: 607).

12. Analysts have long been sensitive to the problems that turbidity can cause in international politics. Note the following passage from Morgenthau's seminal

discussion of the practical problems states encounter in regard to the balance-of-power system.

This uncertainty of all power calculations not only makes the balance of power incapable of practical application but leads also to its very negation in practice. Since no nation can be sure that its calculation of the distribution of power at any particular moment in history is correct . . . the nation must try to have at least a margin of safety which will allow it to make erroneous calculations and still maintain the balance of power. To that effect, all nations . . . must actually aim not at a balance . . . but at a superiority of power. . . . And since no nation can foresee how large its miscalculations will turn out to be, all nations must ultimately seek the maximum of power obtainable under the circumstance. (Morgenthau and Thompson, 1985: 227–228)

13. This perspective on the sociology of the state and its place vis-à-vis society is far from universally accepted. Some development theorists, for example, agree with the basic theoretical premise of the argument but attach far more significance to a country's position within the world economy (e.g., Gerschenkron, 1963; Moore, 1966; Wallerstein, 1974). It is also possible, of course, to account for the nature of domestic structures on the basis of factors that are primarily endogenous to the country in question (see, e.g., Anderson, 1974). My purpose here is not to test the validity of Hintze's proposition but, rather, to simply point out that a collective security system could hold important implications for the nature of state-society relations.

14. I do not address the issues associated with the formation of a collective security system because the institutions comprising Europe's emerging security architecture already have been established. These "sunk investments" have enabled states to avoid the start-up costs typically associated with the formation of international organizations. For our purposes, the more salient issue concerns the ability of CSCE, NATO, and the UN to act on their collective security guarantees.

15. There are, of course, a variety of social and economic sanctions that can be leveled at free riders (Olson, 1965: 60–65; Axlerod, 1986; Martin, 1992). When a member of an institution fails to honor its commitments, for example, the offender may be subject to a set of reputational and other costs that jeopardize its own interests (Keohane, 1984: 83). Theoretically, institutional membership should increase the costs of uncooperative behavior by providing other governments with both the opportunity and the "moral" authority to sanction uncooperative behavior. Technically speaking, however, unless a free rider is expelled from an institution it will still be able to receive a share of the collective benefits.

16. This conceptualization of the "privileged" role the major powers can play in a collective security system should not be confused with a concert-based security system. Conceptually, there are two fundamental differences between collective security and concert-based systems. Whereas collective security systems are characterized by universal membership and a legally binding commitment on the part of governments to respond to any and all acts of aggression, concert systems restrict membership to only the major powers and commit states to do little more than consult with one another in the event of an emergency (Kupchan and Kupchan, 1991).

17. The most comprehensive list of these factors can be found in Kupchan and Kupchan (1991: 144–151). I limit my discussion to the subject of democratization on the part of the major powers because virtually every analyst cites this development as the one factor that has most dramatically increased the possibility of establishing a collective security system in Europe.

18. These factors may be necessary *and* sufficient in regard to the formation of a crisis management regime, however (George, 1988b: 581). If the costs associated

with armed conflict are expected to be prohibitively high, governments will have a clear incentive to try to prevent confrontations from escalating. Under such circumstances, adversaries will share a common interest in containing a war-threatening crisis. This, in turn, will encourage states to try to coordinate their policies and behaviors such that the common aversion (i.e., war) can be avoided. Crisis management, however, constitutes a coordination problem rather than a collaborative game (Miller, 1992). The latter is much more demanding because such situations contain strong incentives to cheat (Stein, 1983: 128).

19. Under conditions of diffuse reciprocity, "an arrangement is expected by its members to yield a rough equivalence of benefits in aggregate and over time" (Ruggie, 1993: 11). For a systematic discussion of the differences between diffuse and strict reciprocity, see Keohane (1989: 132–157).

20. This is, of course, a paradoxical argument. If the interstate system was composed exclusively of democracies, there presumably would be no need for a collective security system. Nevertheless, it does highlight the significance analysts attach to democratization as a factor that can enhance the prospects of establishing a viable system of collective security.

4

DEMOCRACIES, PEACE, AND PARALYSIS

Democracies may not fight one another, but can a group of democratic major powers serve as the minilateralist core of a nascent collective system in post–Cold War Europe? The answer to this question holds important implications for the United States' grand strategy of institutionalization and the future of the European states system. In this chapter, I argue that contemporary systemic and domestic factors are less conducive to the establishment of a collective security system in Europe than most analysts realize.

This counterintuitive claim is premised upon the realist assumption that a state's foreign policy behavior is driven, fundamentally, by a conception of interests (Morgenthau and Thompson, 1985: 1–10; Keohane, 1986: 165). Hence, the potential for international cooperation (as well as for conflict) is inextricably linked to the specific historical circumstances in which states find themselves embedded. On the basis of this conceptualization, it becomes possible to argue that current conditions in Europe will inhibit the major powers from engaging in the collaborative acts that would be called for in a collective security system. This conclusion follows from the simple fact that today's major powers are more secure than major powers have ever been in the history of the European states system. Hence, participating in a collective security system would tend to increase the burdens borne by the major powers without yielding an equivalent increase in the level of their own national securities.

The political salience of this is compounded by the fact that all of the major powers currently are led by democratically oriented governments. To participate in a collective security system, democratic governments will need to mobilize and maintain public support. This dimension of statecraft is crucial within the context of democratic political systems because, as noted previously, liberal norms place the state in a subordinate position vis-à-vis society (Mastanduno, Lake, and Ikenberry, 1989). It is at this juncture that contemporary systemic and domestic conditions combine to diminish the prospects that the major powers will honor the security guarantee that lies at the core of a collective security system. To wit, the benign nature of the major powers' security environment will make it extremely difficult to generate and sustain domestic political support for bearing the costs of multilateral undertakings that promise to yield negligible security benefits. This suggests that under current circumstances, Europe's nascent collective security system is likely to be plagued by repeated acts of involuntary defection (Putnam, 1988: 438) on the part of the major powers. In essence, domestic political constraints will prevent democratic major powers from honoring their pledge to enforce the principles, norms, and rules associated with CSCE, NATO, and the UN.

The purpose of this chapter is to discuss the dilemmas that confront the major powers, especially the United States, when it comes to the issue of European security in the post–Cold War era. I focus on the United States, to the relative neglect of the other major powers, because it constitutes the most powerful member of the institutions that Europe's nascent collective security system comprises. As such, the United States could attempt to play a leadership role that might, in principle, salvage the regime. As I point out, however, the strongest incentives to free ride are likely to be felt on the part of the United States. Hence, U.S. foreign policy makers are likely to be especially prone to adopt a buck-passing strategy when it comes to the management of security problems in Eastern Europe. Obviously, this holds potentially important implications for the future of both the European states system and the grand strategy of institutionalization.

The Sources of Major-Power Security

The major powers of post–Cold War Europe are more secure than states have ever been in the history of the European states system. There are three basic reasons underlying this claim: the advent of nuclear weapons; the declining economic utility of territorial expansion; and the spread of democracy among the major powers. Revolutionary changes in the nature of both military technology and economic production have combined to dramatically lower the expected utility of aggression. Democratization, on the other hand, imposes important restraints on a government's ability to use force as an instrument of foreign policy. Taken together, these factors have diminished the probability of major-power war to its lowest point in the history of international politics. This section examines how each of these factors tends to enhance the security of the major powers.

The nuclearization of the European states system increases stability at the level of the major powers by lowering the expected utility of war between and among these states. Given the destructiveness of nuclear weapons technology, the potential costs of conflict will almost always out-weigh the potential benefits.[1] This should, in turn, breed cautious and con-servative foreign policy behaviors on the part of the major powers that sig-nificantly diminish the likelihood of war between and among them (Jervis, 1989: 23–29).

At present, all but one of the major powers possess this type of mili-tary technology. The lone exception, of course, is Germany.[2] The nuclear capabilities held by the United States, Russia, France, and Britain are listed in Table 4.1.[3]

Table 4.1   Distribution of Nuclear Weapons Among the Major Powers of Europe, 1992

Country	Launchers	Warheads
U.S.	1,239	8,772
Russia	1,857	9,537
France	116	436
Britain	64	96

Source: Stockholm International Peace Research Institute (SIPRI) (1992: 25).

The relative power differentials reflected in Table 4.1 raise obvious questions about the ability of Britain and France to compete with the United States and Russia (see Bobbitt, 1988: 196–199). Politically, how-ever, the significance of nuclear weapons stems from their ability to deter aggression; and this can be done even if an arsenal is technically not ca-pable of surviving a preemptive strike. As Waltz (1983: 583; 1990) argues, to initiate a counterforce attack against a state armed with nuclear weapons, an aggressor must be confident that the operation will render the victim truly unable to retaliate in any meaningful way since even a greatly diminished nuclear force would enable the victim to impose relatively high costs on an aggressor. The logic suggests that even a relatively small nu-clear arsenal can serve as a useful deterrent if a would-be aggressor has doubts about its ability to carry out a disarming first strike (Waltz, 1990: 738).

The difficulties associated with such a mission were highlighted dur-ing the recent Gulf War between Iraq and the United Nations coalition. In this conflict, a consortium of the world's more sophisticated bombers and attack aircraft (i.e., those of the United States, Britain, and France) con-ducted largely unopposed search-and-destroy missions against Iraq's rela-tively small inventory of mobile Scud launchers for over a month. Yet, enough of these launchers survived to enable the Iraqi government to carry out ballistic missile attacks against Israel and Saudi Arabia until the very end of the war. Hence, battlefield dominance on the part of the United Nations coalition did not prevent Iraq from threatening the societal assets of neighboring countries. If Iraq had loaded these missiles with nuclear warheads, it could have imposed high costs on Israel, Saudi Arabia, and other countries even while losing the war in a military sense. This experience obviously holds important implications for any government contemplating a preemptive attack against a state armed with nuclear weapons.

In light of this, it seems prudent to assume that none of the major powers could be highly confident of carrying out a disarming first strike against any of the nuclear powers of Europe. Hence, for analytical purposes, the United States, Russia, Britain, and France all possess the political equivalent of a second-strike capability. Put differently, these states are embedded in a relationship that is commonly referred to as mutual assured destruction (MAD). This form of strategic interdependence obtains if and only if: (1) states are unable to defend their societal assets from nuclear attack, and (2) states possess the retaliatory capabilities to impose high costs on an aggressor (Jervis, 1989: 5–6). Under these circumstances, powerful incentives will exist for cautious and conservative behavior on the part of states.

This conclusion is predicated upon two considerations. First, given the destructiveness of nuclear weapons and the impossibility of defense, nuclear war will be unwinnable in any militarily or politically meaningful sense. Since the possible benefits of aggression will be dwarfed by the risks and potential costs of nuclear conflict, the primary purpose of nuclear weapons becomes deterrence rather than offensive military applications (Brodie, 1946: 17). Second, whenever major military powers become embroiled in a dispute, there is a latent risk of unintentional escalation to all-out war (Jervis, 1989: 21–22, 79–87). This existential threat reinforces deterrence and the need for conservative behavior because of the high absolute costs associated with nuclear conflict. Hence, "even a slight chance that a provocation could lead to nuclear war will be sufficient to deter all but the most highly motivated adversaries" (Jervis, 1989: 38).

As a consequence, the nuclearization of the European states system has served to stabilize and pacify relations between and among the major powers such that the probability of both nuclear and conventional war is extremely low. The Cold War era itself speaks eloquently to this point. Despite the highly competitive nature of the U.S.–Soviet rivalry and the polarization of Europe into competing military alliances, the post–World War II era was characterized by the longest uninterrupted period of major-power peace in the history of international politics (Gaddis, 1987).

Nuclear weapons have created a military environment in Europe characterized by defense-dominance. This refers to a world in which "it is easier to protect and to hold than it is to move forward, destroy and take"

(Jervis, 1978: 187). Under these circumstances, there is little to be gained, and much to be lost, by initiating conflict. Hence, from the standpoint of the major powers, the expected utility of war has diminished significantly. In Kenneth Waltz's (1990: 740) view, this leads to the unavoidable conclusion that "the probability of major war among states having nuclear weapons approaches zero."

Fundamental changes in the nature of economic production also serve to enhance the security of the major powers in post–Cold War Europe. This conclusion stems from the fact that states stand to gain relatively little from territorial expansion within the context of a postindustrial economy (Gilpin, 1981: 219–223; Rosecrance, 1986: 123–133; Mueller, 1989b: 221–223; Kaysen, 1990: 53–57; Van Evera, 1990–1991: 14–16; Kupchan and Kupchan, 1991: 150; Jervis, 1991–1992: 48–50). Hence, there are few economic incentives for the major powers to pursue an expansionist foreign policy that would threaten the political independence and territorial integrity of the states comprising the European states system.

Conceptually, this argument hinges upon the "cumulativity of power resources" (Hopf, 1991: 477–478). If an aggressor can realize significant economic and/or military benefits from seizing control of another state's territory, then the probability of war should increase. Conversely, if the ease with which power resources can be extracted is low, then governments become more likely to refrain from territorial expansion. The cumulativity of power resources varies along with the nature of the factors of production (i.e., land, labor, and capital) that underlie a state's military and economic capabilities in any given era.

Historically, states have been encouraged to expand because of the critical role that territorial control played in regard to the productivity, wealth, and power of an economy. This was especially the case when agriculture constituted the predominant form of economic production (Gilpin, 1981: 110–115). Under this circumstance, states stood to enhance their political power significantly by increasing their territorial extent (Kaysen, 1990: 49). Expansion also was encouraged by the relative ease with which the resources of a conquered territory could be exploited by an aggressor. By seizing control of a piece of land, governments could begin extracting resources almost immediately (Gilpin, 1981: 111; Kaysen, 1990: 49).

The industrial revolution, coupled with the gradual emergence of an integrated world economy, however, slowly began to weaken the linkage between territorial control and economic strength (Kaysen, 1990: 53–57). As Robert Gilpin (1981: 132–133) points out, these developments held out the possibility that "through specialization and international trade an efficient state could gain more than through territorial expansion and conquests." Such opportunities have become even more pronounced as economies move into a postindustrial era wherein information stands as the key to productivity, wealth, and political power (Rosenau, 1990).

Moreover, this emerging mode of production makes it relatively more difficult for an aggressor to exploit the fruits of territorial expansion. The logic underlying this claim is summarized by Stephen Van Evera.

> The shift toward knowledge-based forms of production in advanced industrial economies since 1945 has reduced the ability of conquerors to extract resources from conquered territories. . . . Today's high-technology post-industrial economies depend increasingly on free access to technical and social information. This access requires a free domestic press, and access to foreign publications, foreign travel, personal computers, and photocopiers. But the police measures needed to subdue a conquered society require that these technologies and practices be forbidden, because they also carry subversive ideas. Thus critical elements of the economic fabric now must be ripped out to maintain control over conquered polities. As a result . . . control adds little to national power. (Van Evera, 1990–1991: 14–15)

These fundamental changes in the nature of economic production will serve to diminish the potential for territorial expansion on the part of the major powers in post–Cold War Europe (Van Evera, 1990–1991: 14–15; Kupchan and Kupchan, 1991: 150). This, in turn, also will reduce the likelihood that the major powers will pose a threat to one another's political independence and/or territorial integrity. In essence, the noncumulativity of power resources in contemporary Europe heightens the security of the major powers by lowering the economic incentives to seize and control territory.

In combination, the nuclearization and postindustrialization of the European states system will serve to stabilize and pacify major-power relations because, under these circumstances, "the great powers gain neither more secure borders nor increased wealth by adding more territory" (Goldgeier and McFaul, 1992: 484). Hence, these factors minimize the likelihood of the major powers becoming involved in territorially based disputes. This is important because, historically, territorial issues have been at the center of many of the conflicts that have occurred between and among the major powers.[4]

The significance of this relationship can be highlighted using a data set recently compiled by K.J. Holsti (1991). It lists the primary issues associated with 177 international conflicts spanning the period 1648–1989. Included in the data are thirty-six cases in which at least one major power participated on each side of a dispute.[5] Holsti (1991: 307) identified twenty-four discrete issues that have been associated with two or more of these conflicts. For the sake of simplicity, I have aggregated the data into seven basic issue-areas: territory, economics, systemic maintenance, the creation of states and empires, the preservation of states and empires, the internal political structure of states, and minority rights.[6] By doing so, it is easier to identify the issue-areas most frequently associated with the onset of major-power conflict.

The results of the analysis are reported in Table 4.2. The data confirm that territorial issues have been at the center of more major-power conflicts than has any other issue-area. Historically, disputes concerning the "control, access to, and/or ownership of physical space" (Holsti, 1991: 307) have been present in 69 percent of the armed conflicts that have occurred between and among the major powers.[7] While the salience of this issue-area clearly has been declining over the past four centuries, territorial disputes stand as the one issue most frequently associated with the outbreak of major-power conflict in each of the periods under observation.

Table 4.2   **Frequency of Issue-Areas as a Source of Armed Major-Power Conflict, 1648–1945**

Issue-Area	1648–1714	1715–1814	1815–1917	1918–1945
Territory	75%	83%	50%	33%
Economics	100%	50%	17%	33%
State creation	0%	17%	83%	0%
Internal politics	50%	44%	0%	33%
State preservation	25%	28%	50%	100%
Systemic maintenance	38%	39%	33%	67%
Minority rights	13%	0%	17%	0%

Source: Derived from Holsti (1991).
Note: The twenty-four discrete issues identified by Holsti have been combined into seven distinct issue-areas as follows:

1. Territory: territory, strategic territory, boundaries.
2. Economics: navigation, resources, colonies, protection of nations/commerce.
3. State creation: liberation, secession, unification/consolidation, empire creation.
4. Internal politics: dynastic succession, government composition, autonomy, ideological liberation.
5. State preservation: maintenance of integrity and survival.
6. Systemic maintenance: defense of allies, enforcement of treaties, balance of power, maintenance of regional domination.
7. Minority rights: protection of religious and ethnic beliefs, ethnic unification/irredenta.

This finding reinforces the significance of nuclearization and post-industrialization as factors that will serve to enhance the security of the major powers of Europe. By diminishing the expected utility of territorial expansion, these revolutionary changes in the nature of military technology and economic production decrease the likelihood that the major powers will be motivated to pursue an expansionist foreign policy that would pose a threat to the territorial integrity and political independence of other states.

The prospects for peace and security in post–Cold War Europe also are heightened by the fact that all of the major powers of Europe currently are led by democratically oriented governments. This is an encouraging development because democracies rarely go to war with one another (Russett, 1993). Moreover, democracies are less likely to engage in acts of coercive diplomacy vis-à-vis one another (Maoz and Abdolali, 1989: 21–23). Hence, in terms of their social relations, democracies tend to interact with one another as if they were members of a pluralistic security community (Deutsch, 1988: 272–273). In this type of systemic environment, the security of each state is enhanced because "fears of attack *by one another* are virtually nonexistent" (Keohane and Nye, 1989: 27).

International relations theorists have advanced two basic explanations for the pacific nature of democratic dyads. The first is a normative model of democratic peace that attributes this systemic outcome to the political culture of democracy (see, e.g., Doyle, 1983, 1986). The other is a structural model that emphasizes the institutional constraints that make it difficult for a democratic government to use force as a foreign policy instrument (see, e.g., Bueno de Mesquita and Lalman, 1990; Rummel, 1983; Small and Singer, 1976).

The normative model is premised on the assumption that the foreign policy behavior of states is shaped by the norms of political competition that characterize their domestic political systems (Maoz and Russett, 1993: 625). Hence, the democratic peace could be a function of liberal norms that emphasize the importance of resolving conflicts of interest without resorting to violence (Doyle, 1983: 230). As Maoz and Russett (1993: 625) point out, the political culture of democracy is characterized by a "live and let live" ethos that socializes the citizens of these states to the peaceful resolution of political disputes.[8] To the extent that governments apply these democratic norms to their international interactions, the result should be a relatively pacific pattern of political association in which conflicts of interest do not escalate to the use of military force (Maoz and Russett, 1993: 625).

The structural model, on the other hand, attributes the democratic peace to a variety of institutional restraints that makes it difficult for a liberal regime to pursue an aggressive foreign policy vis-à-vis other democracies. This model is premised, first and foremost, on the fact that liberal regimes need to generate and sustain public support for their foreign policy initiatives (Doyle, 1983: 229).

> International action in a democratic political system requires the mobilization of both general public opinion and of a variety of institutions. . . . This implies that very few goals could be presented to justify fighting

wars in democracies. It also implies that the process of national mobilization for war in democracies is both difficult and cumbersome. (Maoz and Russett, 1993: 626)

The structural model suggests that institutional factors will restrain both the opportunity and the willingness of democratic governments to employ force as a foreign policy instrument, especially when dealing with other democracies. In combination with the normative model, the argument also implies that democracies will be prone to adopt defensively oriented security strategies in which force stands as a weapon of last resort to be used primarily in the name of self-defense (Deudney and Ikenberry, 1991–1992: 86).

These arguments bode well for the security of the major powers comprising the European states system. Democracy is firmly established in the United States, Britain, France, and Germany. Russia, of course, is a newcomer to the democratic tradition; at present, it can best be characterized as a "weakly institutionalized liberal regime" (Snyder, 1989: 6). In light of previous historical experience, one would expect democratization on the part of the major powers to stabilize and pacify the nature of their bilateral and multilateral interactions.[9] This should serve to further diminish the likelihood of major-power conflict in Europe.

This section has reviewed three factors that provide the major powers of post–Cold War Europe with an unprecedented degree of security. Revolutionary changes in the nature of both military technology and economic production have combined to lower the expected utility of territorial expansion. By diminishing the incentives to pursue an expansionist foreign policy, these developments also make it less likely that the major powers will pose a threat to one another's political independence and/or territorial integrity.

The stabilizing and pacifying effects associated with the nuclearization and postindustrialization of the European states system are reinforced by the major powers' embrace of liberal values and institutions at the level of their domestic politics. This will enhance the security of the major powers because: (1) liberal norms socialize democratic leaders to resolve international disputes without resorting to violence, and (2) institutional constraints limit the ability of democratic governments to use force as an instrument of their foreign policy. As a consequence, democratization on the part of the major powers should breed a form of state sociality characterized by a pacific and cooperative pattern of political association.

In combination, these factors have rendered the major powers of contemporary Europe more secure than states have ever been in the history of the interstate system. Indeed, the probability of major-power war in Europe would appear to be at its lowest point since the sixteenth century.

This suggests that the long peace that has characterized the European states system over the past five decades is likely to endure for the foreseeable future.[10] It also implies, however, that the major powers may find it extremely difficult to mobilize and maintain the domestic political support needed to be an active participant in Europe's nascent collective security system.

Democracies and Involuntary Defection

The relative security of the major powers poses a dilemma for these states when it comes to participating in a collective security system. The factors cited in the previous section will serve to diminish the likelihood of major-power conflict in Europe regardless of whether or not a collective security system is established on the Continent. Hence, the security of the major powers is not contingent upon the existence of the regime. To the contrary, their political independence and territorial integrity are underwritten by a combination of technological and political developments that stand independent of any institutional arrangement.

This also suggests that a collective security system is unlikely to enhance the security of the major powers to any significant degree. Given the disincentives to war that presently exist on the part of the major powers, the security guarantees associated with the regime should contribute little, if anything, to the prevention of major-power conflict. Seen from this perspective, a collective security system constitutes an additional layer of insurance that the major powers of contemporary Europe simply do not need in order to be secure.

While a collective security system would yield only marginal benefits to the major powers, the regime would significantly expand the scope of the major powers' security commitments and responsibilities. As noted previously, collective security systems depend heavily upon a minilateralist core of major-power cooperation. In practice, it is the major powers who provide a disproportionate share of the military capabilities that underwrite the institution's security guarantees. Hence, by participating in a collective security system, the major powers would become jointly responsible for managing security issues on a continental-wide basis. Depending upon the level of regional instability, the costs associated with this task could add significantly to the defense burdens that the major powers must bear.

From a rational choice perspective, a collective security system, under contemporary conditions, confronts the major powers with the law of diminishing returns. To wit, each additional increment of managerial effort on their part is unlikely to yield an equivalent increase in the level of their own national securities. In essence, to participate in Europe's nascent collective security system, the major powers must be prepared to bear a disproportionate share of the costs of an institution that will not significantly enhance the security of their own vital national interests.

The salience of this fact is compounded by the domestic political structures that currently characterize the major powers of Europe. Democratization generally enhances the role domestic factors play in the formulation and implementation of public policy (Katzenstein, 1977; Krasner, 1978). Recent research indicates that this proposition holds in the realm of security as well as in other issue-areas (Evangelista, 1989; Barnett, 1990; Snyder, 1991; Risse-Kappen 1991, 1993; Katzenstein and Okawara, 1993).[11] This finding holds potentially important implications for the major powers' ability to serve as the minilateralist core of a collective security system.

To participate in such a system, democratic governments will need to generate and sustain domestic support. This is an essential task within the context of a liberal-capitalist regime because "the state must negotiate with domestic actors for access to [the] societally controlled resources" it needs to pursue a given course of action (Barnett, 1990: 535). Hence, the state must justify its extractive demands by explaining how and why specific policy choices will enhance the nation's security. As Alexander George puts it, policymakers operating within the context of a democratic political system must endeavor to establish and maintain policy legitimacy. In practice, this entails a continuing effort to persuade an array of domestic actors that a particular policy is both desirable and feasible.

It is at this juncture that contemporary systemic and domestic conditions combine to diminish the prospects for major-power participation in Europe's nascent collective security system. Put simply, the extraordinarily benign nature of the major powers' security environment will make it difficult for these governments to convince their respective societies that they should actively support the regime. Since the cause-and-effect relationships linking the security of the major powers to the success of a collective security system are so tenuous under present circumstances, it becomes less likely that democratic governments will be able to convince domestic actors that participation in the regime is warranted.

This is not to suggest that domestic factors will necessarily lead the major powers to boycott a collective security system, as the United States did in regard to the League of Nations during the 1920s. Rather, the argument simply contends that society will be unlikely to authorize the state to expend the manpower, money, and material resources needed to honor the unconditional security guarantee that lies at the core of the regime. In practice, however, this will vitiate the concept of collective security and render such a system politically unviable.

The argument also implies that Europe's nascent collective security system is likely to be plagued by repeated acts of "involuntary defection" on the part of the major powers. Robert Putnam (1988: 438) coined this term to refer to a situation in which domestic political constraints prevent a government from honoring its international commitments. In the present context, involuntary defection would constitute a buck-passing strategy whereby the citizens of one major power seek to pass along the costs of collective security to other states and societies. Such a strategy, however, will jeopardize the political viability of a collective security system by threatening to shatter the minilateralist core of major-power cooperation that underlies this type of regime. In practice, buck-passing is synonymous with the free rider problem.

Christensen and Snyder (1990) argue that the incentive to adopt a buck-passing strategy will vary along with the severity of a state's security predicament. To wit, "the less the vulnerability of states, the greater is the tendency to pass the buck" (Christensen and Snyder, 1990: 145). Conceptually, the authors link the vulnerability of states to two factors located at the systemic level of analysis: the polarity of the international system, and the nature of military technology. Within the context of this analytic framework, Christensen and Snyder (1990: 147) contend that the major powers are most likely to pursue a buck-passing strategy under conditions of multipolarity and defense-dominance.

Both conditions characterize post–Cold War Europe. As noted previously, nuclear weapons technology promotes defense-dominance because of the prohibitive costs associated with this type of major-power warfare (Jervis, 1978: 206–211). Moreover, the dissolution of the Soviet Union has weakened the geopolitical foundations of the bipolar structure that characterized the European states system during the Cold War. While a true multipolar structure may have yet to emerge in Europe, the trend in this direction is unmistakable (Waltz, 1993; Kegley and Raymond, 1993). Hence, the systemic conditions are ripe for the major powers to opt for a buck-passing strategy.

Ironically, the strongest pressures to free ride are likely to be felt on the part of the U.S. government. There are three basic reasons for this. First, the United States is not physically located within Europe. This is an important consideration because the salience of security problems tends to be inversely related to a state's geographical proximity to the source of the problem (Walt, 1987: 23; Buzan, 1991: 135). This suggests that U.S. observers will be more likely than their European counterparts to minimize the significance of instability in post–Cold War Europe because such conflicts will be viewed as holding few immediate and direct consequences for the security of the United States itself.[12] In light of this attitudinal predisposition, one would expect there to be considerable political support within the United States for passing the buck for regional conflict management in Europe to the other major powers.

This preference should be reinforced by the fact that the United States constitutes the most powerful member of the European states system. This suggests that the United States is likely to possess the military and economic strength to defend itself unilaterally from virtually any threat emanating from the region. This possibility is likely to further diminish the value of a collective security system in the eyes of domestic political actors located within the United States as well as their willingness to actively support the institution.

The magnitude of the United States' capabilities relative to its next nearest competitors in Europe is reflected in Tables 4.3 and 4.4. The former reports data for eight states concerning the size of their respective populations, gross domestic product, defense expenditures, and armed forces. The latter table indicates the relative shares of military and economic capabilities possessed by each of these states.[13]

Table 4.3   Distribution of Capabilities in Post–Cold War Europe, 1992

Country	Population (millions)	GDP (trillions)	Defense Expenditures (millions)	Military Manpower (millions)
U.S.	252	5,673	282	1,772
Russia	148	1,112	129	2,720
Germany	80	1,676	31	447
France	57	1,212	35	432
Britain	57	1,018	41	294
Italy	57	1,134	21	354
Ukraine	52	137	68	230
Poland	38	102	2	297

Source: IISS (1992: 13–92).

The last column of Table 4.4 reveals that the United States holds an at least 4:1 advantage over all but one of the members of the European states system. The lone exception, of course, is Russia.[14] Here, the U.S. advantage is merely 1.5:1. In a material sense, the analysis lends additional empirical support to the contention that the United States has emerged from the Cold War as the "world's only remaining superpower" (Nye, 1990; Krauthammer, 1990–1991). As Robert Tucker and David Hendrickson (1992) point out, however, the significance of this oft-repeated claim

Table 4.4   Relative Capabilities of Europe's Major Powers, 1992

Country	% Pop.	% GDP	% Defense Exp.	% Military Manpower	% Total
U.S.	34	47	46	29	39
Russia	20	9	21	41	23
Germany	11	14	5	7	9
France	8	10	6	6	8
Britain	8	8	7	4	7
Italy	8	9	3	5	6
Ukraine	7	1	11	3	6
Poland	5	1	1	4	3

Source: Compiled by author.

stems from more than simply the United States' ranking across some crude measures of national power. It also speaks to the historically unprecedented level of security that the United States has achieved in the post–Cold War era.

> Though threats to the nation's security still had to be anticipated in the post–cold war world, the seriousness of these threats seemed certain to be different from the threats of the last fifty years. Previously the threats had emanated from hostile great powers and encompassed not only a military but an ideological dimension. Following the cold war, the prospective military threats were those of middle and small powers, and no viable ideological challenges were discernible. The great threats to the nation's security—whether physical or ideological—had come to an end with the passing of the cold war. (Tucker and Hendrickson, 1992: 2)

The surplus security that the United States currently enjoys is likely to strengthen the temptation to adopt a buck-passing strategy when it comes time to act upon the commitments associated with Europe's nascent collective security system. For reasons suggested above, U.S. foreign policy makers are likely to have a difficult time mobilizing domestic political support for an active U.S. role in multilateral military operations that can do little to improve upon the United States' already impressive level of security. The geographic distance separating the United States from the source of regional instabilities in Europe will further complicate the prospects for convincing domestic actors that U.S. security interests warrant the state's involvement in such conflicts.

The preferences held by domestic groups and coalitions are of considerable importance to the conduct of U.S. security policy because the structure of the U.S. political system affords members of society ample opportunities to influence the policymaking process (Risse-Kappen, 1993: 241–242). This is the third, and final, reason why the United States is likely to pursue a buck-passing strategy in post–Cold War Europe.

A country's domestic political structure can be characterized in terms of three basic factors: (1) the centralization of its political institutions and decisionmaking processes; (2) the polarization of society and the degree to which groups can be mobilized politically; and (3) the nature of the policy networks linking state and society (Risse-Kappen, 1993: 241). On the basis of this analytic framework, a country can be located along a continuum of state-society relations that ranges from "state-dominated" to "society-dominated" structures.[15] In theory, a country's position along this continuum will provide an indication of the extent to which a state is likely to be sensitive and responsive to societal demands and preferences in the realm of security (Risse-Kappen, 1991: 484–486).

Conceptually, the U.S. political system lies closer to the society-dominated end of the continuum (Ikenberry, Lake, and Mastanduno, 1988: 219–243). Its institutions are fragmented both constitutionally (Henkin, 1972) and bureaucratically (Allison, 1971). As a consequence, the U.S. government is characterized by a relatively decentralized decisionmaking process that provides numerous actors with multiple points of access (Risse-Kappen, 1993: 242). This creates ample opportunities for societal groups and coalitions to channel their demands into the political system (Destler, Gelb, and Lake, 1984). It also increases the likelihood that policymakers will be sensitive and responsive to public preferences because the viability of a policy option often will hinge upon the ability of political elites to mobilize and maintain the support of actors located in society (Waltz, 1967; Cohen, 1973; Leigh, 1976; George, 1980–1989; Snyder, 1991: 255–294; Deese, 1994). Hence, in theory, the structure of the U.S. political system should enhance the ability of societal groups and coalitions to influence policy outcomes in the area of security (Risse-Kappen, 1991: 493).

This is an important consideration within the context of the present discussion because the actors comprising U.S. society are deeply divided when it comes to the use of force as an instrument of U.S. foreign policy. This fact renders a commitment by the United States to participate in a collective security system inherently problematic. In the absence of a national consensus in favor of contributing U.S. military forces to multilateral missions, the U.S. government is likely to face strong incentives to opt for a buck-passing strategy in the name of avoiding a contentious, and potentially costly, domestic political debate.

The divisions characterizing U.S. society over the use of force are reflected in a recent study by Eugene Wittkopf (1990). Using data derived from public opinion surveys conducted by the Chicago Council on Foreign Relations during the period 1974–1986, Wittkopf (1990: 25–26) identifies four distinct foreign policy belief systems: internationalist, conservative, accommodationist, and isolationist. Moreover, these attitudes are evident in the structure of beliefs held by both the general public and the elite members of U.S. society (Wittkopf, 1990: 116).

As Wittkopf (1990: 50) points out, these groups were divided on the basis of their underlying attitudes toward: (1) communism, (2) relations with the Soviet Union, and (3) the use of U.S. military forces abroad. Obviously, the dissolution of the Soviet Union has all but eliminated the first two issues as a source of contention in U.S. foreign policy. This suggests that the use of force is likely to become the defining issue of public debate during the post–Cold War era. If this is the case, then the prospects for establishing a national consensus in favor of participating in a collective security system are bleak. This conclusion stems from the fact that since the end of the Vietnam War, the people of the United States have been generally reluctant to support military interventions (Wittkopf, 1990: 228–234).

The enduring strength of this so-called Vietnam syndrome is reflected in Table 4.5, which indicates how members of the general public have been distributed across the foreign policy belief systems noted above. In general, questions pertaining to the use of force have tended to pit internationalists and conservatives against a tacit alliance of accommodationists and isolationists (Wittkopf, 1990: 29). As the percentages reported in Table 4.5 suggest, these blocs have been about evenly matched over the past two decades.

Table 4.5   Distribution of U.S. Society Among Four Types of Foreign Policy Belief Systems, 1974–1986 (percentage)

Belief System	1974	1978	1982	1986
Internationalist	29	29	28	28
Conservative	23	22	24	24
Accommodationist	27	26	26	24
Isolationist	22	22	22	24

Source: Derived from Wittkopf (1990: 26).

This balance of societal forces, however, is unlikely to persist in the post–Cold War era (Yankelovich, 1992: 9). Conservatives, in particular, are likely to become much more selective in their support for military interventions. During the Cold War, conservatives tended to favor the use of force because of their overriding concern with the threat of Soviet expansionism (Wittkopf, 1990: 29–32). In the absence of this clear and present danger, it seems likely that conservatives will approach the question of intervention in much the same way that isolationists traditionally have. When vital U.S. interests are at stake, and the use of force promises to be decisive in securing these interests, then conservatives and isolationists are both likely to support the deployment of U.S. military forces (Schneider, 1992: 63–64). In situations that do not meet these criteria, however, neither group is likely to favor the use of force, especially if it entails getting involved in the internal affairs of another country (Jentleson, 1992).

This tacit alliance between conservatives and isolationists, combined with the accommodationists' congenital opposition to the use of force, suggests that there is likely to be a solid majority of U.S. citizens who will not favor military interventions as a standard operating procedure on the part of its government in the post–Cold War era. Given the openness of the U.S. political system, it also is likely that decisionmakers will be cognizant of these attitudes and responsive to them.

Obviously, this does not bode well for active U.S. participation in Europe's nascent collective security system. The relative security of the United States in the post–Cold War era, coupled with the ability of societal actors to press their demands on the state, suggests that U.S. foreign policy makers will face considerable domestic pressure to adopt a buck-passing strategy when it comes to the management of European security problems.

Nor is the United States likely to be unique in this regard. All of the major powers of Europe are embedded in the same relatively benign international security environment. While Russia, Germany, France, and Britain certainly will be more sensitive to regional instabilities than will the United States (due to their geographic proximity), sensitivity is not the same as vulnerability (Keohane and Nye, 1989: 11–19). And in the latter respect, the political independence and territorial integrity of these countries are more secure from external attack today than they have ever been in their history.

Moreover, all of the major powers comprising the European security system are presently characterized by domestic political structures that afford societal groups and coalitions unprecedented opportunities to influence the decisionmaking process. Under present circumstances, the members of these societies seem likely to demand that their respective governments attend to an array of domestic problems that were allowed to fester during the Cold War era, rather than expend resources in military undertakings that can do little to enhance the security of their country.

This combination of systemic and domestic factors is not encouraging when it comes to the future of a collective security system in post–Cold War Europe. The argument suggests that the regime is likely to be plagued by repeated acts of involuntary defection on the part of the major powers. This possibility, in turn, will serve to undermine both the credibility and the efficacy of the institutions comprising Europe's emerging security architecture.

> Multilateral orders are more credible if countries believe the political leadership of the major power(s) is subject to significant domestic constraints on defecting from the rules of the multilateral order. . . . While other devices may also enhance credibility, domestic political factors are virtually indispensable. (Cowhey, 1993: 160–161)

The Significance of the War in Bosnia

The problems outlined in the preceding section have all become manifest in the major powers' response to the war in Bosnia. I conclude this chapter with a brief discussion of the conflict's significance as a harbinger of the dilemmas that the major powers are likely to confront when it comes to the multilateral management of security problems in Eastern Europe and the former Soviet Union.

Bosnia stands as a painful reminder that war has not become obsolete even in Europe. This distressing fact should disabuse us of the notion that Western civilization has somehow progressed to the point where war has become unthinkable. This hopeful thesis has been advanced recently by some international relations theorists who argue that war is fundamentally a social practice, analogous to dueling and slavery, that has been delegitimized throughout much, if not all, of the developed world (Mueller, 1989b; Ray, 1989). The war in Bosnia provides stark evidence that this transformative process is, at best, incomplete. Under the right circumstances, the men and women of contemporary Europe remain quite capable of killing one another in the name of achieving their political objectives.

Some observers seek to obscure this point by attributing the war in Bosnia to ancient ethnic and religious animosities. This shrouds the conflict in the mist of history and, hence, enables us to depict the war as an atavism holding little relevance for the future of post–Cold War Europe. While comforting, this stance is ultimately an act of mystification that seeks to diminish the war's significance by invoking a historical legacy of prejudice and hatred that presumably stands beyond the pale of human control (Snyder, 1993).

While there is indeed such a legacy, this should not be allowed to obscure the fact that the protagonists in this conflict have made a conscious decision to commit horrific acts in the name of furthering their political interests. The atrocities associated with the war in Bosnia—ethnic cleansing, rape as an instrument of political influence, the systematic torture of unlawfully imprisoned foreign nationals, and repeated attacks against undefended civilian populations—have not happened simply because of a primordial predisposition to violence. This path was chosen deliberately by men and women who are as much a product of modernity as they are an echo of the past. In the final analysis, the Bosnian conflict, like so many of the conflicts that have occurred during the course of European history, is firmly rooted in a set of rational calculations about the political utility of violence, coercion, intimidation, and terror.

Our interest in Bosnia, however, stems from more than its stunning human costs. The conflict also has a symbolic significance that has not been lost on contemporary observers. The following statement by Secretary of State Warren Christopher is indicative of the importance that statespeople and scholars alike have attached to the war in Bosnia.

> This conflict may be far from our shores, but it is certainly not distant from our concerns. We cannot afford to ignore it. . . . The continuing destruction of a new United Nations member challenges the principle that internationally recognized borders should not be altered by force. . . . There is also a broader imperative here. The world's response in the former Yugoslavia is an early and crucial test of how it will address the concerns of the ethnic and religious minorities in the post–Cold War period. That question reaches throughout Eastern Europe and the former Soviet Union . . . and it reaches to other continents as well. . . . Bold tyrants and fearful minorities are watching to see whether "ethnic cleansing" is a policy the world will tolerate. (Christopher, 1993d: 76)

Given this conception of the principles at stake in Bosnia, the failure of CSCE, NATO, the UN, and the European Community to resolve this conflict has proven to be a deeply frustrating experience. Nor is Bosnia an isolated case. These institutions also have been unsuccessful in their attempts to manage similar conflicts in Croatia, Azerbaijan, Georgia, and Tajikistan. In essence, multilateral management has proven unequal to the task of dealing with Europe's most pressing security problems.

These repeated failures, of course, can be attributed to a variety of factors. Some are intrinsic to this particular type of political violence. Such disputes, for example, typically center on intractable territorial claims and the political disposition of isolated ethnic communities; moreover, the protagonists also tend to be highly motivated individuals driven, in part, by hypernationalism (Posen, 1993). At the same time, however, international conflict management in post–Cold War Europe clearly has been complicated by the major powers' unwillingness to use force in support of their diplomatic efforts. This problem is most evident in the case of Bosnia.

Over the past two years, the major powers have taken concerted steps to try to resolve the Bosnian conflict on several different occasions (Steinberg, 1993). In May 1993, for example, the United States, Russia, Britain, and France announced a joint action program designed "to help extinguish this terrible war and to achieve a lasting and equitable settlement."[16] This initiative, like similar efforts on the part of CSCE, NATO, and the UN, ultimately was unsuccessful.

A number of analysts account for this disappointing performance by pointing to the major powers' refusal to get directly involved in the Bosnian conflict as military combatants (e.g., Ramet, 1992; Pfaff, 1993). While the major powers have been willing to coordinate their policies in an attempt to resolve the war, these initiatives have been limited to the realm of diplomatic overtures and the application of economic sanctions. At no time have the major powers come close to using force in an attempt to actually bring the fighting to an end.[17] The aforementioned joint action program, for example, was a compromise basket of initiatives arrived at following the failure of the major powers to agree on a plan that would use force to coerce the Bosnian Serbs to accept a political settlement (Williams, 1993a: A40). Put differently, the major powers' concerted efforts in regard to Bosnia and other conflicts in Europe have always stopped short of direct military intervention.

This self-restraint, however, has tended to emasculate diplomatic efforts undertaken by the United Nations, CSCE, and the European Community. In essence, these institutions have been deprived of the coercive instruments that are sometimes needed to induce compliance with the generalized principles of conduct that stand at the core of multilateral institutions (Martin, 1993: 101–103). Hence, in the case of Bosnia, the institutions comprising Europe's nascent collective security system have been placed in the awkward position of having to accept territorial aggression on the part of Serbia and Croatia as the price to be paid for reaching a settlement (Pfaff, 1993: 104–105). In the words of one embittered UN official, this experience holds a sobering lesson for the future of multilateral undertakings: "[T]he international community should not intervene unless it is ready to pay a high price in blood and resources" (Preston, 1993: A39).

The comment is instructive because it highlights the dilemma a collective security system is likely to face repeatedly in post–Cold War Europe. To wit, the regime is premised upon a level of major-power commitment and cooperation that may not be politically viable under contemporary systemic and domestic conditions. This is likely to be an especially nettlesome problem in situations such as Bosnia where the major powers are called upon to undertake so-called peace enforcement missions. This, of course, is simply another name for military interventions conducted under the auspices of a multilateral institution. Since such initiatives represent the most potentially costly tool associated with the task of regional conflict management, we should expect this type of collaborative effort to generate the strongest incentives for the major powers to opt for a buck-passing strategy. Obviously, this possibility jeopardizes both the effectiveness and the durability of Europe's emerging security architecture.

> Given the pathetic performance of Western countries in the Bosnia crisis, the proposal suffers from a massive credibility problem. Why should anyone in Eastern Europe take such a guarantee seriously? Why should they believe that it was any more than a bluff, something done in the hope that the commitment itself would be an effective deterrence and with no serious intention of honoring it? (Harris, 1993: 43)

Matters are further complicated in this regard by certain historical legacies that can inhibit the major powers from assuming an active role in the management of Eastern European conflicts. As James B. Steinberg points out, this has been a continuing problem in the case of the war in Bosnia.

> Because many states in the region had historical alliances or adversary relations with the parties to the Yugoslav conflict, their impartiality as mediators was questioned. Russia, France, and to a lesser extent, the United Kingdom were viewed as sympathetic to Serbia, while Germany's support for recognizing the independence of Croatia and Slovenia was attributed to past political, cultural, and religious ties. Some . . . even hinted darkly about German designs to establish a "Fourth Reich." (Steinberg, 1993: 61)

This is an important consideration given the expansionist tendencies that Germany and the Soviet Union have exhibited in regard to Eastern Europe during the twentieth century. This imperial tradition, which actually dates back to the nineteenth century, is likely to make the members of the European states system wary of actively encouraging Germany and Russia to deploy a significant number of their military forces in the region. Indeed, the United States' official position in regard to Russian peacekeeping operations within Europe is to oppose any mission that would create an opportunity for Russia to "suppress regimes or political groups that are hostile to Russia" (Smith, 1993: A1).

This policy is outlined in Presidential Decision Directive 13 (PDD-13), which was leaked to the press in August 1993. It indicates that the Clinton administration will not support United Nations' resolutions that would authorize peacekeeping operations composed predominantly of Russian forces; nor will the United States vote in favor of Russian requests for financial assistance in support of such operations (Smith, 1993: A1).

PDD-13 even specifies six criteria that the Clinton administration will use to decide whether or not to support UN peacekeeping operations involving a significant number of Russian troops.

As might be expected, the policy has drawn the ire of the Russian government. In a speech to the UN General Assembly, for example, Russia's foreign minister, Andrei Kozyrev, declared that when it comes to conflicts involving the countries comprising the former Soviet Union, "no international organization or group of states can replace our peacekeeping efforts" (Williams, 1993c: A25). Similar sentiments were expressed by Kozyrev in an op-ed piece that appeared shortly thereafter in the *Washington Post*.

> Admittedly, partnership—and over the long term, alliance—with the United States and the West is a natural choice for a democratic Russia. But this does not mean a confluence. We do have and shall continue to have our special interests, different from Western interests and at times even competing. . . . [We will not disregard] the special responsibility devolving on Russia in the Eurasian geopolitical space. Protection of legitimate rights of Russian-speaking minorities in the former Soviet republics, the economic reintegration of the republics and peace-making activities in conflict areas: All of these are an objective necessity. (Kozyrev, 1993: C7)[18]

This discussion suggests that Germany and Russia may be asked to contribute fewer military forces to multilateral missions than will the other major powers. This also implies that the fate of Europe's nascent collective system is likely to hinge upon the willingness of the United States, France, and Britain to actively support the regime. Given the United States' reluctance to deploy ground forces in Bosnia, even in support of humanitarian relief efforts, the prospects for a major U.S. contribution in situations requiring the use of force are not encouraging. If anything, the United States appears poised to return to the free riding strategy that characterized its foreign policy during the first half of the twentieth century. I will address this issue and the implications it holds for the United States' grand strategy of institutionalization in the next chapter.

Conclusion

"A democracy," de Tocqueville (1969: 229) once wrote, "finds it difficult to coordinate the details of a great undertaking and to fix on some plan and carry it through with determination in spite of obstacles." This aphorism frequently is invoked by scholars seeking to account for the sudden twists and turns of U.S. foreign policy (e.g., Kennan, 1951). But what implications does this insight hold for a group of democracies thrown together by the vicissitudes of the post–Cold War era?

This is a critical issue within the context of the United States' grand strategy of institutionalization because of the importance U.S. foreign policy makers attach to multilateral institutions as tools for the management of European security affairs. The argument advanced in this chapter suggests that the effectiveness of Europe's nascent collective security system will be undermined by the interaction between (1) the major powers' relatively benign security environment, and (2) the domestic structures that presently characterize these countries. In essence, this combination of systemic and domestic conditions heightens the probability that Europe's emerging security architecture will be little more than a facade engraved with solemn pledges that lack practical significance.

Notes

1. Presumably, there are at least a few political goals worth dying for. I would characterize this as the "Patrick Henry syndrome." The reference, of course, is to the apocryphal story of the American Revolutionary leader who defied his British captors with the well-known line, "Give me liberty or give me death." In theory, such highly motivated individuals could find the costs of nuclear war to be outweighed by the potential benefits.

2. Germany renounced its right to manufacture, possess, or control nuclear, biological, and chemical weapons in the treaty relating to the unification of the country in September 1990.

3. For the purposes of this discussion, the nuclear weapons located on Ukrainian territory have been eliminated from the analysis. As noted in Chapter 2, Ukraine has pledged to become a non-nuclear state by the end of this decade.

4. There have been relatively few systematic studies of the role that issues play as a source of international conflict (Levy, 1989: 227). At present, the most comprehensive empirical analysis of the subject can be found in Luard (1986). Diehl and Goertz (1988) have examined the relationship between territorial changes and militarized conflict.

5. Altogether, major powers have been involved in 122 of the cases contained in the data set. Since our interest here is limited to the subject of conflict between and among the major powers, I have ignored the 86 cases featuring a confrontation between a major power and a minor state. The states qualifying as major powers over the past four centuries have been identified on the basis of lists compiled by Levy (1983: 197) and Waltz (1979: 162).

6. The discrete issues comprising each issue-area are listed at the foot of Table 4.2.

7. It is also interesting to note that, historically, the major powers have tended not to get involved in armed conflicts over "minority rights" issues. This issue-area also ranks last among the triggers associated with the outbreak of direct major-power conflict. This finding should serve to allay concerns about a major-power confrontation emerging from a dispute over issues pertaining to ethnic and/or religious minorities in the post–Cold War era.

8. The violence plaguing U.S. society, of course, raises some doubts about this argument. In theory, liberal norms should exert their strongest effects within the United States, as it is the world's oldest and most firmly established democracy. Yet, U.S. citizens commit more acts of violence against one another than do the citizens of any other industrialized country. An explanation for this tendency is not intuitively obvious within the context of the peace-through-political-culture hypothesis.

9. For a critique of the peace-through-democratization thesis, see Mearsheimer (1990: 48–51). In essence, Mearsheimer (1990: 50) argues that "history provides no clear test of [the] theory" that democratization on the part of the major powers will breed enduring peace and stability in Europe. This is a somewhat ironic position for Mearsheimer to take considering the significance he attaches to nuclear deterrence as the foundation for European stability during the Cold War era. As numerous scholars have pointed out, history provides few unambiguous tests of deterrence theory either (see Lebow and Stein, 1989).

10. Previous periods of long major-power peace within Europe occurred during 1815–1853 and 1871–1914. Unfortunately, no one has ever undertaken a systematic, comparative analysis of this phenomenon (Spiezio, 1992). As a result, we have yet to develop a theoretical framework that might account for this recurrent systemic outcome. This is troubling because, in the absence of a comparative analysis, it is logically impossible to establish cause-and-effect relationships in international politics (Most and Starr, 1989: 13).

11. The influence domestic factors exert appears to vary across issue-areas, but it is nonetheless present in all realms of public policy.

12. Historically, the most salient threat to U.S. security emanating from Europe has been posed by a major power's attempt to dominate the Continent militarily (Morgenthau, 1951/1989). Since contemporary conditions greatly diminish the probability that a major power will undertake such an aggressive and expansionist foreign policy, one could argue that there are few, if any, regional threats that could seriously jeopardize the security of the United States.

13. The analysis is based upon the widely used index of national power developed by Singer, Bremer, and Stuckey (1972).

14. The analysis also lends further empirical support to Waltz's (1993: 52) recent contention that, despite the dissolution of the Soviet Union, the structure of the European states system can still best be characterized as bipolar.

15. In a "state-dominated" structure, the policymaking process is insulated from societal demands; hence, the state enjoys a high degree of autonomy vis-à-vis society. In a "society-dominated" system, on the other hand, the state is highly susceptible to public opinion because the decentralized nature of the decisionmaking process provides societal actors with opportunities to channel their demands into the political system (Risse-Kappen, 1991: 484–485).

16. The text of the joint action program can be found in *Foreign Policy Bulletin* (July/August 1993) 4:13–15.

17. NATO did pledge to enforce the no-fly zone that the United Nations established over Bosnia in October 1992. This has done little to enhance the credibility of the major powers' commitment to use force as an instrument of international conflict management, however. A recent UN report indicates that there have been 674 violations of the zone since NATO was authorized to shoot down military aircraft over Bosnia. NATO commanders, however, have requested permission to use force on only one occasion (Preston, 1993: A10).

18. This assertion of Russia's "special responsibility" in regard to the countries comprising the former Soviet Union is significant because Kozyrev is a member of the most pro-Western group inside of Russia (Arbatov, 1993: 9). Other groups vying to influence the course of Russian foreign policy tend to be much more nationalistic and hostile toward the West. The coalition led by Gennadiy Zhirinovsky, for example, "is devoted to the goal of revival of the Russian empire . . . [and is] prepared to reinstate the Soviet Union by military force" (Arbatov, 1993: 14). Zhirinovsky caused a stir throughout Europe when his Liberal Democratic Party received 23 percent of the vote in Russia's December 1993 parliamentary elections.

5

THE UNITED STATES
AND THE ISOLATIONIST IMPULSE

The grand strategy of institutionalization represents an ambitious attempt on the part of the United States to nurture the development of a liberal international society in Europe. The ultimate goal is to construct a regional political order wherein the exercise of state power would be constrained by an interlocking network of liberal norms and institutions located at the level of both domestic and international politics. The attractiveness of this design lies in its potential for creating the political foundation for an enduring era of peace and prosperity in Europe.

In pursuit of this goal, U.S. foreign policy makers have taken steps to promote the democratization and marketization of state-society relations in countries located throughout Eastern Europe and the former Soviet Union. At the same time, the United States also has supported efforts to broaden and deepen the role international institutions play in the management of regional security, economic, and social issues. In combination, these initiatives represent the key components of a long-term, integrated strategy designed to facilitate the emergence of a common normative and institutional framework in Europe that, ultimately, will serve to liberalize the constitutive principles of political association both within and between states.

The values and assumptions underlying the grand strategy of institutionalization have long been a part of the U.S. diplomatic tradition. They are reflected, for example, in Woodrow Wilson's famous Fourteen Points speech, which indicated how self-determination, open commerce, and collective security could serve to enhance the relative peace, stability, and welfare of post–World War I Europe. The same celebration of liberal values and institutions can be found in the "four freedoms" that Presidents Roosevelt and Truman would cite as central to their efforts to reconstruct the European states system in the aftermath of World War II (McCormick, 1985: 3–62).

These parallels are instructive because they also highlight a fundamental choice that stands before U.S. foreign policy makers in the post–Cold War era. For the third time this century, the United States is confronted with the task of redefining the security-related role it will play in regard to the European states system. The past offers two models of the direction that U.S. foreign policy makers could take. The first stems from the post–World War II era and is characterized by active U.S. involvement in the day-to-day management of European security affairs. The second harkens back to the interwar period when the United States refused to assume such burdens.

In this chapter, I present evidence that indicates that the United States is on the verge of adopting an isolationist policy in regard to the countries of Eastern Europe and the former Soviet Union. The analysis suggests that in the future U.S. foreign policy makers are likely to adopt a buck-passing strategy when it comes to the management of security issues in Eastern Europe. This approach, however, will not be identical to the isolationism that characterized U.S. foreign policy during the first half of the twentieth century.

Whereas in the past the United States abstained from any military involvement in Europe, the evidence presented in this chapter suggests that the United States will remain active in this region, but its managerial activities will be limited to the western half of the Continent. That is, the United States will remain a member of NATO, but it will not extend binding security commitments to countries located in the eastern half of the Continent; nor will the United States be an active participant in multilateral military interventions undertaken in this part of Europe. In essence, U.S. foreign policy makers in the post–Cold War era will seek to combine elements of both containment and isolationism in their approach to European security.

Obviously, this Janus-faced approach holds important implications for the future of both the European states system and the United States' grand strategy of institutionalization. As noted previously, the United States' post–Cold War strategy is premised upon the same basic approach that it took toward Western Europe in the decades following the end of World War II. In both cases, the United States has promoted democracy, markets, and international institutions as the keys to achieving peace and prosperity in Europe.

There will be, of course, one fundamental difference between then and now. As a result of the Cold War, the United States was willing to make an explicit collective security commitment to the market democracies of Western Europe. This was codified in the North Atlantic Treaty, which extended an unconditional U.S. security guarantee to the political autonomy and territorial integrity of its allies. In the post–Cold War era, however, the United States has refused to make a similar commitment to the emerging market democracies of Eastern Europe and the former Soviet Union. The most U.S. foreign policy makers have been willing to offer is a

"Partnership for Peace" that establishes a pledge on the part of the United States to consult with Eastern European governments in the event of regional instability but stops far short of the binding security commitment the United States adopted in regard to the countries of Western Europe.

The question, of course, is whether or not the United States' unwillingness to underwrite the security of Eastern European countries will jeopardize the success of its long-term strategy in Europe. What implications will the absence of a credible collective security framework hold for the prospects of transforming the European states system into a pluralistic security community overlaid by a single, integrated market? The present chapter addresses this issue and assesses the consequences that an isolationist stance toward Eastern Europe may hold for the future of the European states system under present systemic and domestic conditions. I begin by presenting evidence that indicates that the United States is on the verge of adopting an isolationist posture when it comes to the management of international security issues in the eastern half of the Continent.

The United States and Isolationism

"Isolationism" is a politically charged word that frequently is used without a great deal of analytical precision. It is a term of opprobrium that typically is invoked in public debates in an attempt to paint an opponent as hopelessly naive about the realities of contemporary international politics. In this caricature, isolationists are routinely depicted as individuals who would have the United States abstain from all involvement with the outside world. It is this vision of an autarchic United States, insulated from the vicissitudes of international politics, that presumably lies at the core of the isolationist agenda.

Like all caricatures, however, this representation grossly exaggerates the practical implications that have been associated with an isolationist approach to U.S. foreign policy. The United States has practiced isolationism throughout most of its history (Crabb, 1986: ch. 1). Indeed, it was the dominant paradigm of U.S. foreign policy until World War II. During the reign of isolationism, however, the United States never attempted to withdraw completely from international affairs. To the contrary, the United States has been an active participant in international politics from the very beginning of the Republic (DeConde, 1963). This is especially the case in regard to the United States' foreign economic policy (Williams, 1962). Hence, there is little empirical support for the contention that isolationism can be understood simply in terms of a desire for autarchy.

Isolationism, however, does have special significance within the context of the United States' approach to regional security issues outside of the Western Hemisphere. As Robert Tucker (1972: 32) points outs, isolationism historically has been synonymous with an unwillingness on the part of the United States "to entertain certain relationships, notably alliances, and undertake certain actions, notably interventions." Put differently, "the issue of isolationism continues principally to turn, as it has always turned, on the willingness [of the United States] to enter into . . . military commitments" (Tucker, 1972: 36–37).

This conceptualization suggests two empirical referents that can be used to assess the extent to which U.S. foreign policy makers are being guided by the precepts of isolationism: (1) an unwillingness to extend binding security commitments to other states, and (2) an unwillingness to participate in military interventions. In addition, Tucker also identifies a cognitive factor that has been closely associated with an isolationist posture on the part of the United States.

> What distinguishes an isolationist outlook . . . is the conviction that sustained foreign involvement—and particularly one holding out the constant prospect of military intervention—poses a grave threat to America's institutions and well-being. An extreme sensitivity to, and consequently an obsessive fear of, the domestic effects of foreign policy has been one the hallmarks—perhaps *the* hallmark—of the isolationist outlook. (Tucker, 1972: 35)

In its classical manifestation, isolationism was characterized by an unwillingness on the part of the United States to: (1) establish peacetime security commitments with other countries, (2) permanently station its military forces outside of U.S.–held territories, or (3) use force in support of the status quo in either Europe or Asia (Art, 1991: 6). At the same time, however, this posture did not prevent U.S. foreign policy makers from taking part in multilateral efforts to deal with international security problems. During the interwar period, for example, the United States was willing: to participate in multilateral arms control negotiations; to consult with other governments in response to crises; to undertake diplomatic efforts in the name of resolving international conflicts; and even to participate, on occasion, in multilateral economic sanctions imposed against states that had committed acts of aggression (Paterson, Clifford, and Hagan, 1991: 314–332, 335–348).

Throughout this period, however, U.S. foreign policy makers also made it clear that the United States would not guarantee the political autonomy or territorial integrity of any country; nor would the United States intervene militarily in Europe or Asia unless another major power appeared to be on the verge of establishing a predominant position within the region (Tucker, 1972: 28). In essence, the United States framed itself as the defender of last resort in regard to the security of both these regional systems. While isolationism did not completely rule out the possibility that the United States would use force in support of its interests in Europe and Asia, it did significantly limit the range of strategic exigencies that would warrant such a response.

As this discussion implies, it would not be inconceivable for contemporary U.S. foreign policy makers to participate in the multilateral institutions comprising Europe's emerging security architecture while simultaneously adopting an isolationist approach to the management of European security affairs. In practice, such a policy would be characterized by a tendency on the part of U.S. foreign policy makers to pledge their unequivocal support for the principles, norms, and rules that lie at the core of these institutions, while also taking steps to minimize or reduce the security-related costs that the United States has to bear in regard to these commitments. The remainder of this section presents evidence that indicates that the United States is indeed moving in this direction when it comes to the security of countries located in Eastern Europe and the former Soviet Union.

There are four pieces of evidence that suggest that U.S. foreign policy makers are on the verge of adopting an isolationist stance toward countries located in the eastern half of the Continent. The first can be found, ironically, in the Clinton administration's Partnership for Peace program. As discussed in Chapter 2, this program is designed to promote "a practical working relationship" between NATO and the other members of the European states system (Christopher, 1994: C7). President Clinton (1994: A11) also has framed this initiative as a clear demonstration of "America's commitment to Europe's safety and stability." Yet, the program actually contributes little to the security of countries located in Eastern Europe and the former Soviet Union.

The United States and its NATO allies, for example, are under no obligation to defend the political autonomy or territorial integrity of these states. Nor is there any commitment to ultimately admit these states to NATO at some point in the foreseeable future. At the same time, however, these "partners" will be expected to make a material contribution to NATO peacekeeping operations in Europe (Christopher, 1993b: 55). This creates an obvious opportunity for the United States to pass along the costs of these missions (especially in the form of manpower) to Eastern European states. Seen from this perspective, the following comment by former Secretary of Defense Les Aspin takes on added significance.

> Partnership for Peace requires that partners make a real contribution. It doesn't just ask what NATO can do for its new partners, it asks what the new partners can do for NATO. *Security consultations, for instance, will be available to active partners, those who make a contribution and*

involve themselves in the multinational activities that are the heart of NATO. (Aspin, 1993: 4; emphasis added)

The exploitative potential implicit in the program is enhanced considerably, of course, by the fact that the United States (in conjunction with its allies) will judge the eligibility of prospective members, in part, on the basis of "each candidate's ability—as demonstrated through Partnership for Peace—to take on the mutual defense responsibilities of member states" (Christopher, 1994: C7). In essence, this initiative presents U.S. foreign policy makers with the best of both worlds. It entitles them to put claims on the resources held by Eastern European states without requiring the United States to establish a binding commitment to the security of these countries.

A second piece of evidence can be found in the Combined Joint Task Force, which was created by NATO during its January 1994 summit in Brussels. In essence, this institutional innovation will permit the United States to abstain from NATO peacekeeping operations in Eastern Europe. The task force provision frees member states from any obligation to contribute troops to a NATO mission undertaken outside of Western Europe (Williams and Hockstader, 1994: A16). Hence, the United States would be entitled to participate in the decisionmaking process relating to such missions, but it also would be under no obligation to provide U.S. forces in the name of implementing the decision.

Obviously, the Combined Joint Task Force agreement creates yet another opportunity for the United States to adopt a buck-passing strategy when it comes to the task of international conflict management in Eastern Europe. This possibility has not gone unnoticed. An unnamed, senior-level British official warned that the arrangement could "turn out to be a disguise for covert American withdrawal" from the alliance's newly established mandate for peacekeeping in Europe (Drozdiak, 1994: A32). Similar sentiments were expressed by at least some members of the State Department. In fact, one foreign service officer, not speaking for attribution, characterized the entire summit as "a disguise for U.S. withdrawal from Europe" (Williams, 1994: A32).

These concerns are warranted because the task force agreement basically institutionalizes the free riding behavior that the United States has exhibited in regard to the war in Bosnia. Over the past two years, several members of NATO have provided ground forces in support of the United Nations' peacekeeping and humanitarian efforts in Bosnia. France and Britain have contributed the largest contingents (approximately 6,000 and 2,500 troops, respectively); lesser contributions have come from countries such as Canada, Spain, the Netherlands, and Italy. U.S. foreign policy makers, however, have refused to deploy any ground forces in the country until after a peace settlement has been arranged.[1] In the meantime, the United States' contribution has been limited to the provision of cargo planes and fighter aircraft that have been used to deliver humanitarian relief supplies and to help enforce the no-fly zone over Bosnia.

The Combined Joint Task Force agreement would permit the United States to duplicate this "division of labor" in all subsequent peacekeeping and peace enforcement missions undertaken by NATO. In principle, however, the agreement goes even further than that: It formally excuses the United States from contributing any military forces to NATO operations outside of Western Europe. As such, it provides U.S. foreign policy makers with a legitimate justification for not bearing the costs of international conflict management in Eastern Europe.

A third piece of evidence can be found in a series of major addresses delivered by President Clinton and other senior-level policymakers in September 1993. The speeches were intended to outline the United States' approach to UN peacekeeping operations. They also reveal, however, that the Clinton administration is distancing itself from the generalized principles of conduct that lie at the core of the United Nations.

In an address to the General Assembly, for example, President Clinton exhorted the United Nations to become much more selective when it comes to acting upon the security-related responsibilities specified in Article 1 of the Charter.

> The United Nations simply cannot become engaged in every one of the world's conflicts. If the American people are to say yes to UN peacekeeping, the United Nations must know when to say no. (Clinton, 1993c: 52)

The passage is significant because it represents an obvious departure from the principle of unconditionality that stands as the hallmark of a collective security system. As John Gerard Ruggie (1993: 11) points out, this type of institution is based upon a commitment to action that members are expected to abide by "without regard to the particularistic interests of the parties or the strategic exigencies that may exist in any specific occurrence." The president's comment, however, suggests that the United States will eschew this freestanding commitment in favor of a case-by-case approach that differentiates situations on the basis of the administration's evaluation of their relative importance to the maintenance of international peace and security.[2]

A similar theme was sounded by Anthony Lake during a major foreign policy address delivered at Johns Hopkins University. Lake concluded his discussion of the Clinton administration's grand strategy by elaborating on the United States' attitude toward multilateralism.

> Let me say a word about the current doctrinal debate on multilateralism. . . . For any official with responsibilities for our security policies, only one overriding factor can determine whether the U.S. should act multi-

laterally or unilaterally, and that is America's interests. We should act multilaterally when doing so advances our interests—and we should act unilaterally when that will serve our purpose. (Lake, 1993: 44–45)

While this axiom of prudential statecraft certainly makes intuitive sense from the standpoint of a domestic audience, it also is at odds with the principled commitments that accrue to the members of a collective security system. As noted in Chapter 3, this type of regime "requires its participants to renounce temporary advantages and the temptation to define their interests narrowly in terms of national interests" (Caporaso, 1993: 56). The speeches cited above, however, constitute a public renunciation of these norms of behavior. They also provide an indication that U.S. foreign policy makers will orient themselves to the institutions comprising Europe's nascent collective security system on the basis of a utilitarian calculation of the relative costs and benefits a proposed multilateral undertaking holds for the national interests of the United States.

The fourth, and final, piece of evidence suggesting that the United States will adopt an isolationist stance toward Eastern Europe can be found in the mood of its people. National mood is an elusive, but a potentially useful, concept that refers to the underlying values, assumptions, and beliefs that characterize a society at any given historical moment (Almond, 1960). Its political significance stems from the law of anticipated reactions, which holds that decisionmakers will forgo certain foreign policy options if they think the public is likely to withhold support for, or actively oppose, an initiative (Kegley and Wittkopf, 1991: 253, 300). This argument parallels V. O. Key's (1961) contention that mass opinion can influence the policymaking process by establishing certain parameters that can serve as a constraint on a government's ability to act both domestically and internationally.

Assessing the national mood of a society is laden with methodological challenges. Survey data compiled since the end of the Cold War, however, indicate that the people of the United States have become deeply concerned about their economic security and remain wary of military interventions, especially when they entail involvement in the internal affairs of other countries (Schneider, 1992). Writing on the eve of the 1992 election, for example, pollster Daniel Yankelovich noted that

over the past year the public's level of anxiety has been rising steadily. What worries Americans is that the economy is growing stagnant or declining (75 percent), that Japan is ahead of the United States in terms of its ability to compete (77 percent) and that as a consequence the American standard of living is in grave danger. The main source of voters' anxiety is not the recession as such, . . . they fear that something is fundamentally wrong with the U.S. economy. (Yankelovich, 1992: 2)

This is not to suggest that economic concerns are prompting a desire on the part of U.S. citizens to withdraw from international politics. Indeed, the latest (1990) Chicago Council on Foreign Relations survey reveals that 61 percent of the general public believes that it is important for the United States to continue playing a leadership role in world affairs (Schneider, 1992: 41).[3] Hence, the issue is "not *whether* the United States should be involved abroad, but *how* that involvement should be pursued" (Wittkopf, 1990: 27; emphasis added).

And, when it comes to this instrumental question, the U.S. population exhibits a clear preference for reducing the United States' share of the costs associated with the task of managing international security problems. The Chicago Council survey, for example, indicates that the majority of the general public is in favor of cutting back the amount of military (73 percent) and economic (61 percent) assistance that the United States grants to other countries (Schneider, 1992: 56). This represents a 10–15 percent increase over the number of U.S. citizens favoring aid reductions in the 1986 survey. Moreover, a plurality of the general public also supports further reductions in U.S. defense spending as part of a broader effort to shrink the size of the federal government's budget deficit (Schneider, 1992: 55).

These preferences can be linked, at least in part, to an underlying belief that security-related expenditures jeopardize the health of the United States' economy. In a 1988 survey conducted by the Americans Talk Security (ATS) Project, 1,004 registered voters were asked if the United States damages its economy by spending money to defend other countries. A resounding 86 percent of the respondents agreed with this proposition (ATS, 1988: 84). This sentiment also is reflected in the fact that 81 percent of the people were in agreement with the statement that the United States "can't afford to defend so many nations" (ATS, 1988: 101).

It is clear that most of the voters surveyed regard Japan and the countries of Western Europe as the primary beneficiaries of the United States' efforts in the realm of security. Of the respondents in the ATS poll (1988: 89), 84 percent agreed that Japan and Europe "are winning the economic competition" because of the billions that the United States spends to defend them. This perception also would seem to underlie the general public's contention that the United States' allies can and should do more to provide for their own security (ATS, 1988: 100).

Surveys indicate that the United States' people also are reluctant to support the use of military forces abroad, especially if the mission threatens to be lengthy, costly, and indecisive (Jentleson, 1992: 72). It is interesting to note that the United States' success in the Gulf War had little appreciable effect on the public's appetite for military interventions. In a poll taken two days after the end of the war, for example, 60 percent of the respondents indicated that this experience had *not* increased their willingness to support the use of U.S. military forces in an attempt to solve international problems (Schneider, 1992: 64). A majority of the people also are not in favor of becoming involved, militarily, in the internal affairs of other countries. In a CBS News–*New York Times* poll conducted in March 1991, 60 percent of the people surveyed expressed their opposition to U.S. involvement in such situations (reported in Schneider, 1992: 66–67). Overall, the data contained in these surveys indicate that the public's current attitude toward the use of force has not changed significantly from what it has been throughout the post-Vietnam era (see Wittkopf, 1990: 174–181).

As this discussion suggests, the mood of the U.S. people currently is characterized by a deeply entrenched wariness about its country's involvement in military interventions and a relatively more recent concern about the future of U.S. economic strength. In combination, these anxieties have dampened the public's willingness to have the United States serve as the world's police in the post–Cold War era (Yankelovich, 1992: 9). This also has prompted a number of U.S. citizens to express an interest in enhancing the role international institutions play in the management of international security problems (Yankelovich, 1992: 10–11). In the 1990 Chicago Council survey, for example, a plurality of both the general public and the elite opinion-makers were in favor of strengthening the United Nations to this end (Schneider, 1992: 42–43).

Public support for a multilateralist solution to the problem of international conflict management, however, should not be confused with a willingness on the part of the people to bear a disproportionate share of the costs associated with these institutions. In fact, there are reasons to suspect that the allure of these institutions lies in their capacity to serve as a redistributive mechanism whereby the United States actually can diminish the size of its contribution to the maintenance of international peace and security.

This has certainly been a popular theme with Bill Clinton. As a presidential candidate, for example, Clinton frequently stressed the need for a more equitable burden-sharing arrangement on the part of the United States and other members of the UN.

> America needs to reach a new agreement with our allies for sharing the costs and risks of maintaining peace. While Desert Storm set a useful precedent for cost-sharing, our forces still did most of the fighting and dying. We need to shift that burden to a wider coalition of nations of which America will be a part. (Clinton, 1991: 5)

In a speech to the Foreign Policy Association, Clinton returned to this theme and elaborated on the policies he would pursue as president in an attempt to redistribute the United States' share of the costs associated with collective security.

> We can make these institutions more effective and sustainable by reapportioning the burden of collective security. . . . We should seek to reduce our 30 percent financial share of U.N. peacekeeping operations to the 25 percent we pay for the U.N.'s regular budget. . . . Japan and Germany should be made permanent members of the U.N. Security Council. And we should seek larger contributions from those with the greatest interest in particular efforts. . . . We [also] should look to our alliances to take a more active role in the defense of their own regions. (Clinton, 1992a: 12)

Since taking office, the Clinton administration has continued to emphasize the value of international institutions as redistributive mechanisms that can lighten the security burdens borne by the United States in the post–Cold War era (Albright 1993b: 32; 1993a: 33–35). During his Senate confirmation hearings, for example, Secretary of State designate Warren Christopher announced that the United States

> will not turn [our] blood and treasure into an open account for the use of the rest of the world. . . . It will be our administration's policy to encourage other nations and the institutions of collective security, especially the United Nations, to do more of the world's work to deter aggression, relieve suffering, and keep the peace. (Christopher, 1993e: 10)

Moreover, the Clinton administration has made it clear that the United States is unlikely to be a frequent participant in multilateral military interventions. National Security Adviser Anthony Lake made this point explicit in his aforementioned address at Johns Hopkins:

> While there will be increasing calls on us to help stem bloodshed and suffering in ethnic conflicts, and while we always will bring our diplomacy to bear . . . there will be relatively few intra-national ethnic conflicts that justify our military intervention. (Lake, 1993: 44)

Additional evidence, of course, can be found in the United States' approach to the conflicts in Bosnia and Somalia. As noted above, the United States has refused to intervene at all in the Bosnian war. This is a striking decision on the part of the Clinton administration because, as Lake (1993: 42) himself acknowledges, the conflict is being fought in the heart of a region that is of critical importance to the success of the administration's "strategy of enlargement." The Somalian case, however, may be even more instructive when it comes to assessing the United States' attitude toward military interventions in the post–Cold War era. In essence, the Somalia situation demonstrates how sensitive the people of the United States and Congress have become to the costs of using force abroad in affairs where vital U.S. interests are not directly at stake.

On October 3, 1993, a contingent of U.S. Army Rangers was ambushed by members of a Somalian militia on the streets of Mogadishu. In the ensuing battle, twelve U.S. soldiers were killed, eighty servicemen were wounded, and at least one pilot was taken prisoner. The engagement sparked an immediate confrontation between the Clinton administration and members of Congress over the United States' involvement in Somalia. The opposition was led by Senator Robert Byrd, who previously had signaled the depth of his unease over the United States' policy in regard to the conflict in Somalia during a Senate debate on September 8.

> Mr. President, it is becoming increasingly unclear as to what useful purpose is being served by the presence and operation of these forces in Somalia. . . . The cost to the United States of this mission is 44 million a month—that is, about a half-billion dollars a year. . . . The Congress never considered, was never asked, and certainly has never approved of United States participation in [this mission]. . . . U.N. Security Council resolutions have never, and should never serve as a substitute for the responsibility of this institution [i.e., Congress] to affirmatively approve placing U.S. forces into hostile situations. I see in the front of this Chamber the U.S. flag. I do not see in front of this Chamber the UN flag. (Byrd, 1993: 20)

The death of twelve U.S. soldiers was enough to prompt Senator Byrd to call for the withdrawal of all U.S. forces from Somalia by the end of 1993. The incident also led sixty-five members of the House of Representatives to send a letter to President Clinton demanding an end to the United States' involvement in the UN mission (Dewar, 1993a: A39). Perhaps most important, the crisis also motivated several senators to propose resolutions that would have required the president to obtain explicit congressional authorization before U.S. troops could participate in future multilateral peacekeeping operations (Marcus and Dewar, 1993: A1).

Ultimately, these resolutions were abandoned in favor of a compromise position that simply "urges" President Clinton to seek congressional approval before U.S. troops are used in support of future UN operations (Dewar, 1993b: A1). Nevertheless, the backlash generated by the loss of a dozen U.S. lives in Somalia provides a startling indication of how sensitive Congress and the people are to the costs of military intervention when vital U.S. interests are not at stake. We also should note that this domestic political opposition ultimately did lead the Clinton administration to reverse its policy in regard to the United States' involvement in the Somalian conflict. On October 7, President Clinton announced that "all American troops will be out of Somalia no later than March the 31st [1994]" (Clinton, 1993a: 34).

This section has presented evidence that indicates that the United States is exhibiting isolationist-like tendencies when it comes to the task of international conflict management in Eastern Europe. In both words and deeds, U.S. foreign policy makers have repeatedly signaled their unwillingness to: (1) establish binding security commitments to the countries of Eastern Europe and the former Soviet Union, or (2) participate in military interventions within the Continent. As noted above, this approach to regional security issues in Europe corresponds closely to the foreign policy practices that historically have been associated with isolationism in U.S. foreign policy.

Moreover, the Clinton administration's inclination to refrain from assuming new security-related burdens in Europe is reinforced by an underlying sense of economic insecurity on the part of the people of the United States. This pervasive feeling of anxiety has prompted societal groups and coalitions to demand that the United States government devote the bulk of its attention and resources to an array of pressing domestic problems. In essence, the end of the Cold War has elevated socioeconomic concerns to the top of the United States' foreign policy agenda. Within this context, additional security responsibilities on the part of the United States would constitute an unwelcome distraction that might also jeopardize the state's capacity to address the fears and concerns of its people.

This sentiment, of course, is shared by President Clinton, whose victory in the 1992 election was due, in no small part, to his realization that "it's the economy, stupid." Clinton's (1991: 2) conviction that the United States is "a military giant crippled by economic weakness and an uncertain future" has prompted his administration to subordinate security issues to the task of "mobilizing our country for the global economic competition that is the hallmark of this new age" (Clinton, 1992b: 14). Indeed, Secretary of State Christopher (1993e: 10) has pledged that the administration will "harness our diplomacy to the needs and opportunities of American industries and workers" in the post–Cold War era. As Robert Tucker (1972: 35) points out, the economization of the U.S. foreign policy agenda also has been closely associated, historically, with the emergence of an isolationist approach on the part of the United States.

Isolationism and the Grand Strategy of Institutionalization

To mention isolationism, of course, is to invoke historical memories of the calamities that befell Europe, Asia, and the rest of the world when the United States adopted this approach in the 1920s and 1930s. The interwar period stands as perhaps the darkest episode in the history of U.S. foreign policy. By shunning involvement in European and Asian security affairs, the United States undeniably did contribute to a sequence of events that culminated in the deadliest war in world history—a global conflict leading to the deaths of tens of millions of people.

Understandably, this experience has had a lasting effect upon the way scholars and statespeople alike think about isolationism. In essence, this approach to the issue of regional security in Europe (and elsewhere) has become synonymous with the height of folly and irresponsibility on the part of U.S. foreign policy makers (Morgenthau 1951/1989: 637–640). It is for this reason that the term "isolationist" is regarded as one of the most damnable labels in the lexicon of U.S. political discourse.

Hence, we must be careful when using this term to characterize the Clinton administration's approach to post–Cold War Europe. That is, we should not exaggerate the scope of the isolationist impulse in contemporary U.S. foreign policy. There is no evidence to suggest, for example, that the Clinton administration is on the verge of abrogating the United States' commitment to NATO; nor are U.S. foreign policy makers contemplating the withdrawal of all U.S. troops from the Continent. President Clinton made this clear in a speech he delivered during the January 1994 NATO summit in Brussels.

> I have come here today to declare and to demonstrate that Europe remains central to the interest of the United States. . . . That is why I am committed to keeping roughly 100,000 American troops stationed in Europe. . . . It is not habit, but security that justifies this continuing commitment by the United States. (Clinton, 1994: A11)

There are few reasons to doubt the sincerity of the United States' commitment to NATO or the security of its long-standing Western European allies. In its approach to the security of countries located in Eastern Europe and the former Soviet Union, however, the Clinton administration is exhibiting quite definite isolationist tendencies. And this is a matter of considerable importance within the context of the United States' grand strategy of institutionalization because these are the countries that must be transformed if Europe is to become a genuine "democratic international society." As it stands, however, it would appear that these states and societies will have to navigate the twin processes of democratization and marketization bereft of the collective security guarantees that the United States extended to the countries of Western Europe during the post–World War II era.

Conceptually, this highlights an important point about the role systemic factors play in shaping the conduct of U.S. foreign policy. The United States has been promoting democratization, marketization, and integration as the solution to Europe's enduring security problems throughout the twentieth century. Yet, it was only in the post–World War II era that U.S. foreign policy makers opted to play an active role in the day-today management of European security issues. This era, of course, was characterized by bipolarity. This was a systemic context that encouraged the United States to make a legally binding and freestanding commitment to the security of countries located in Western Europe and elsewhere.[4] As Kenneth Waltz has argued, bipolarity exerts this effect because

> in a bipolar world there are no peripheries. With only two powers capable of acting on a world scale, anything that happens anywhere is potentially of concern to both of them. Bipolarity extends the geographic scope of both powers' concern. It also broadens the range of factors included in the competition between them. (Waltz, 1979: 171)

The structural effects associated with bipolarity stand in sharp contrast to the security implications that confront states within the context of a multipolar structure. When three or more major powers exist, the clarity of the threat environment states must deal with diminishes considerably. This heightens uncertainty on the part of decisionmakers about "who is a danger to whom, and who can be expected to deal with threats and problems" (Waltz, 1979: 170). Put differently, multipolarity dampens a state's willingness to undertake managerial tasks relating to the maintenance of international peace and security because in this systemic environment "dangers are diffused, responsibilities unclear, and definitions of vital interests easily obscured" (Waltz, 1979: 171).[5]

These considerations are relevant to the present discussion because history reveals that U.S. foreign policy makers have always opted for an isolationist approach to European security issues under conditions of multipolarity. Hence, we should not be surprised that the Clinton administration is exhibiting this tendency in regard to the countries of Eastern Europe and the former Soviet Union. This predisposition is being driven by structural factors that have exerted quite similar effects throughout the course of U.S. history.

This implies, of course, that the dilemmas confronting the United States when it comes to the issue of European security in the post–Cold War era do not stem from the Clinton administration's naïveté or its failure to internalize the lessons derived from the United States' disastrous experience with isolationism in the 1920s and 1930s. Nor is it a reflection of the administration's inability to articulate a coherent vision of the future. Rather, the dilemma confronting the Clinton administration is rooted in a combination of systemic and domestic factors (i.e., multipolarity, defense-dominance, and a society-dominated policy network) that creates strong incentives for the United States to adopt a buck-passing strategy when it comes to the management of security issues in Eastern Europe. This problem would exist regardless of who was elected president in the 1992 election.

This also suggests that U.S. aspirations are likely to far exceed the resources the United States is actually willing to commit when it comes to implementing the grand strategy of institutionalization. The existence of such a gap between the means and the ends of strategy is nothing new, of course, within the context of U.S. foreign policy. Indeed, this type of insolvency has been a problem since the earliest days of the Republic (Lippmann, 1943; Huntington, 1987–1988). In recent years, however, the means-ends gap has reached epic proportions in the United States. As Robert Tucker points out, this may well be Ronald Reagan's most enduring legacy as president.

> There is perhaps no more venerable tradition in American foreign policy than that of willing ambitious ends while refusing to entertain the necessary means. What distinguished Mr. Reagan in this respect was that he carried a very old tradition to new heights. To an extent that is probably without precedent, he has severed the connection between ends and means in foreign policy. What is more, *it is this very disjuncture that has formed the essential element of his reconstituted domestic base.* From the outset, the great appeal of the president's policies was that they demanded so little of the public while promising so much. . . . [Reagan] has transformed what had been a predisposition not to pay for the American position in the world into something close to a fixed resolve not to do so. If there is a consensus today in foreign policy, this must be regarded as its central tenet. (Tucker, 1988–1989: 27; emphasis added)

There are signs that Bill Clinton is following in Reagan's footsteps (Samuelson, 1994: A19).[6] The president has articulated a vision of the United States, and of the world, that is more ambitious than any administration's since Franklin Roosevelt's. After two years in office, however, it remains unclear whether the current United States government possesses either the capacity or the competence to effect such fundamental changes at home or abroad. This unavoidably raises a question about the Clinton administration's ability to exert leadership at the level of both domestic and international politics.

This is a matter of considerable importance within the context of the United States' grand strategy of institutionalization because recent research indicates that leadership is an indispensable factor when it comes to the creation of regimes and durable international political orders (Rapkin, 1987; Ikenberry and Kupchan, 1990; Young, 1991). I conclude the section with a brief discussion of this issue and the implications U.S. isolationism may hold for the prospects of building a "democratic international society" in Europe.

Oran Young (1991) has elaborated on the critical role that leadership plays in regard to the success of institutional innovation by developing a typology that highlights the distinctive contribution different forms of leadership make to the process of regime formation. Intellectual leaders, for example, provide the ideas and knowledge that explain why a particular institutional arrangement would be useful for dealing with a specific collective action problem (Young, 1991: 298–300).[7] Entrepreneurial leaders, on the other hand, make an invaluable contribution to the politics of regime creation through their ability "to foster integrative bargaining and to put together deals that would otherwise elude" governments (Young, 1991: 293–295). Finally, structural leaders can facilitate the task of institutional innovation by either: (1) bearing a disproportionate share of the costs associated with the regime's operation, or (2) manipulating its material resources in ways that coerce other states into subsidizing the regime (Young, 1991: 289–291).[8]

Young (1991: 303) hypothesizes that at least two forms of leadership must be exercised if states are to create a viable international institution. A recent study by Ikenberry and Kupchan (1990) provides empirical support for this proposition, but the analysis also suggests that structural leadership is an absolutely necessary condition for the creation of a durable international order. Put differently, regime formation may entail different types of leadership, but historical experience indicates that a structural leader must be present if the effort to create an international institution is to succeed (Ikenberry and Kupchan, 1990: 314–315).

The authors base this conclusion on several case studies taken from the twentieth century. Of interest here is their analysis of the United States' efforts to rebuild the European states system in the aftermath of World Wars I and II. In both cases, the fate of the United States' postwar strategy hinged on the willingness of U.S. foreign policy makers to supplement their intellectual and entrepreneurial leadership with tangible offers of economic and military assistance to the countries of Europe (Ikenberry and Kupchan, 1990: 295–307). In essence, previous historical experience indicates that when it comes to the promotion of liberal values and institutions in Europe

> normative persuasion is insufficient to drive the socialization process. Elites in secondary states come to believe in the norms and ideals articulated by [U.S. foreign policy makers] only in junction with the provision of material incentives or through the imposition of those norms via direct intervention. (Ikenberry and Kupchan, 1990: 314)

This discussion highlights the importance of the means-ends gap that has come to characterize U.S. foreign policy over the past decade; it also underscores the significance of the isolationist tendencies that the United States is exhibiting in regard to the countries of Eastern Europe and the former Soviet Union. In essence, both issues are indicative of an unwillingness on the part of U.S. foreign policy makers to exercise the type of leadership that has proven to be decisive in past U.S. attempts to transform Europe into a "democratic international society."

This possibility, of course, was forewarned in May 1993 by Undersecretary of State Peter Tarnoff, who was quoted as saying that the Clinton administration "expects to withdraw from many foreign policy leadership roles customarily assumed by the U.S." (Williams and Goshko, 1993: A1). While this position was quickly disavowed by Warren Christopher (1993f), actions do speak louder than words. And in this sense, the recent course of U.S. foreign policy has been consistent with Tarnoff's contention that

> [w]e simply don't have the leverage, we don't have the influence, the inclination to use military force. We don't have the money to bring positive results anytime soon. (Williams and Goshko, 1993: A1)

The United States' unwillingness to exert structural leadership in regard to Eastern Europe and the former Soviet Union raises the obvious question of who will take on this responsibility. Given the combination of systemic and domestic factors confronting Germany, France, and Britain, it seems unlikely that they—singularly or in combination—will be enthusiastic about the prospects of assuming the role of structural leader in Europe. Indeed, only Russia has expressed an unequivocal commitment to the task of international conflict management in Eastern Europe.

As noted previously, the Russian government already has asserted a "special responsibility" in regard to peacekeeping operations in the countries comprising the former Soviet Union. More recently, Foreign Minister Kozyrev has indicated his support for maintaining a Russian military presence in at least some of these republics. In a January 1994 interview with the *Washington Post*, Kozyrev suggested that Russia "should not withdraw from those regions which have been in the sphere of Russian interest for centuries" (Hiatt, 1994: A21). Russia also has signed a collective security agreement with six other members of the Commonwealth of Independent States (Hiatt, 1992: A16). Hence, Russia is formally committed to defend Armenia, Georgia, Kazakhstan, Turkmenistan, Uzbekistan, and Tajikistan from external attack. It is not inconceivable, therefore, that Russia would be willing to expand the scope of its managerial efforts to include countries located in Eastern Europe as well.

Such a development is bound to raise security concerns on the part of the United States and its Western European allies. An assertive Russia, however, is not necessarily a bad thing. Historically, the stability of the European states system has been enhanced considerably when Russia has assumed an order-keeping role in the eastern region (Bunce, 1993). It is not by coincidence that two of the longest uninterrupted periods of major-power peace in Europe (i.e., 1815–1853 and 1871–1914) have been characterized by an active Russian role in the day-to-day management of Eastern European security affairs. This stability, of course, has been purchased at a considerable cost to the states and societies comprising this region. The Russian tradition is not rooted in the liberal values and institutions that characterize the "West." And until Russia becomes a firmly established market democracy, it will be difficult to estimate what consequences the expansion of Russian influence in Eastern Europe will hold for the United States' grand strategy of institutionalization.

Conclusion

It is customary for books such as this to conclude either by speculating about the course of future events or by offering a set of policy prescriptions that would address the problems outlined in the study. However, given the formidable problems associated with the task of forecasting in international politics (Jervis, 1991–1992; Gaddis, 1992–1993), I will break with this tradition in favor of a more modest approach: outline the outstanding issues raised in this study and reiterate their significance from the standpoint of both U.S. foreign policy and international relations theory.

"Politics," Max Weber once wrote, "is a strong and slow boring of hard boards" (quoted in Gerth and Mills, 1946: 128). The practitioners of the grand strategy of institutionalization would do well to keep this axiom in mind. The collapse of the Soviet Union, coupled with the bankruptcy of Marxist-Leninist ideology, has created a unique opportunity for the promotion of liberal values and institutions in Europe. The success of this effort, however, is not foreordained by some unassailable force of historical evolution. Such liberal conceit is no more defensible than the smugness that Marxists used to exhibit in regard to the future of international politics. There is nothing inevitable about the direction that the European states system ultimately will take in the post–Cold War era. Like virtually all political phenomena, the fate of Europe lies more in the realm of choice than of necessity.

This conviction underscores the importance I have attached to the problems and possibilities associated with the task of implementing the grand strategy of institutionalization. The United States' post–Cold War strategy represents an ambitious attempt to transform the way hundreds of millions of people define their identities, interests, institutions, and principles of international political association. Obviously, this transformative process will take years, if not decades, to complete, just as it did in the case of Western Europe. The potential benefits, however, are enormous.

If successful, the strategy would lay the domestic political foundation for the emergence of a liberal international society in Europe. This would not only benefit Europeans. It also would serve U.S. security and economic interests by diminishing the potential for war and revolution in Europe. Such a development would enable the United States to forgo the costly military interventions and high levels of defense expenditures that have characterized U.S. policy throughout much of the twentieth century. Moreover, marketization and regional integration promise to create new opportunities for the expansion of U.S. exports to the Continent. This is of considerable importance given the role that international exchange has assumed as a catalyst for growth and development on the part of the U.S. economy.

This vision, of course, is tinged with an undeniable element of Wilsonian utopianism. The grand strategy of institutionalization envisions a world in which autocracy, militarism, imperialism, and war have been reduced to the level of historical curiosities; a world in which the law of the jungle has been replaced by the rule of law; a world that ultimately stands beyond the pale of power politics. Obviously, it is relatively easy to dismiss this vision as yet another manifestation of the systemic innocence that has characterized U.S. foreign policy since the earliest days of the Republic.

Such cynicism must be tempered, however, by an appreciation of the remarkable transformations that occurred in Western Europe during the post–World War II era. This experience suggests that while the construction of a liberal international society in Europe is difficult, it is not impossible. Hence, the vision outlined by the Bush and Clinton administrations represents more than simply another bout of wishful thinking on the part of U.S. foreign policy makers. It is an approach that is rooted, ultimately, in five decades of successful Western experience.

To acknowledge the possibilities of achieving similar transformations in Eastern Europe and the former Soviet Union is not to argue that the United States' post–Cold War strategy is destined to succeed due to the sheer weight of the Western European model. The political, economic, and social challenges associated with the process of liberalizing former communist countries are simply too daunting to have a great deal of confidence when it comes to predicting the ultimate outcome of this transitional stage of development. While the zeitgeist of international politics clearly lies in the direction of democracy and markets, we have seen these waves of liberalization crest and recede before (Huntington, 1991). Again, there is nothing inevitable about the power of liberalism as a world historical force. As with any ideology, there are always alternatives possessing their own hegemonic pretensions.

This is to suggest that the fate of the European states system is unlikely to be decided anytime soon. During this interregnum, however, the United States clearly has an opportunity to influence the course of events. While U.S. foreign policy makers can support the process of liberalization in Eastern Europe and the former Soviet Union in a number of different ways, we should not overlook the important contribution collective security institutions made to the transformation of Western Europe into a pluralistic security community during the post–World War II era. A reassuring environment can have a significant and long-lasting effect upon the nature of states and societies. No nation should appreciate this more than the United States.

Europe's nascent collective security system has the potential to provide the Continent's weakly institutionalized liberal regimes with the sense of security they will need in order to become firmly rooted market democracies. To be effective, however, the multilateral institutions comprising Europe's emerging security architecture also will require sustained U.S. leadership. Unfortunately, it is unclear whether the Clinton administration possesses the skill or the will to meet this demand either at home or abroad. Leadership is in short supply in the contemporary United States; we have been reduced to a nation of managers.

This point also raises an issue that should be of considerable interest to international relations theorists. Democracy is a powerful force in contemporary international politics. Scholars have long recognized this fact, and we are quite right to emphasize the many benefits associated with the spread of liberal values and institutions. At the same time, however, we should not minimize or ignore the more troubling implications associated with the advance of democracy.

While it is true that democracies rarely go to war with one another, it is not at all clear that democracies can cooperate in the realm of international security management. I have attempted to underscore this point through an extended discussion of the factors that may inhibit today's democratic major powers from actively supporting Europe's nascent collective security system. The present study, however, has done little more than scratch the surface of this question. Before we jump to any conclusions about the (in)ability of democracies to engage in far-reaching acts of international security cooperation, we need to investigate a considerably broader range of cases.

Such an effort could make a valuable contribution to our understanding of the future of world politics. We have entered an era that is unprecedented in the history of the interstate system. Never before have so many of the world's major powers been characterized by liberal norms and institutions at the level of their domestic politics. There are, of course, compelling reasons to believe that this development should significantly improve the prospects for global peace and prosperity. We would be remiss, however, if we did not acknowledge that democratic political systems are characterized by a degree of parochialism and self-centeredness that creates an inherent tension among the members of a liberal society. It would be surprising to find that such problems do not exist at the level of international relations.

Notes

1. The United States, however, has sent 500 soldiers to Macedonia in an attempt to deter Serbia from invading the country.

2. The Clinton administration's turn toward a policy of selective engagement becomes even more remarkable if it is contrasted with the plea for unconditionality contained in a speech delivered by Ambassador Albright to the Council on Foreign Relations in June:

> If the Security Council is to speak and act on behalf of the entire world community, its efforts cannot be confined to only those issues of greatest consequence to its richer members. (Albright, 1993a: 34)

3. In contrast, only 55 percent of the general public in the 1974 survey thought it was important for the United States to continue playing a leadership role in world affairs (Schneider, 1992: 41).

4. Hence, the United States' efforts to transform Western Europe into an integrated, pluralistic security community during the Cold War era cannot be attributed primarily to some ideological predisposition "to remake the world in the American image" (Burley, 1993: 129). Rather, U.S. efforts in regard to this region were driven largely by the strategic exigencies associated with the emerging bipolar confrontation between the United States and the Soviet Union (Weber, 1992).

5. As noted previously, the incentives to shirk managerial responsibilities in a multipolar system also will increase if the balance of military technology is seen as favoring the defense (Christensen and Snyder, 1990).

6. This makes intuitive sense since the Reagan years demonstrate that a president can make exaggerated promises to the people, and repeatedly fail to make good on such commitments, without suffering retribution at the polls. Ironically, this appears to be one lesson that George Bush did not learn during his tenure as vice president. While it is always risky to account for an electoral outcome on the basis of a single factor, it seems clear that Bush's defeat in the 1992 election was primarily a result of his refusal to make any meaningful promises in regard to "fixing" the economy or leading the United States out of the recession (Duffy and Goodgame, 1992: 273–274).

7. In Young's analytic framework, leaders typically are individuals. In the case of intellectual leadership, however, an "epistemic community" presumably could serve in this capacity as well. For a discussion of epistemic communities and the role they can play in the process of regime formation, see Haas (1992).

8. This conception of leadership corresponds closely to the one found in the literature on hegemonic stability theory (see Keohane, 1989: 74–100; Modelski, 1978; Gilpin, 1981; Snidal, 1985).

BIBLIOGRAPHY

Books and Journal Articles

Allison, G. T. 1971. *Essence of Decision: Explaining the Cuban Missile Crisis.* Boston, Mass.: Little, Brown.

Almond, G.A. 1960. *The American People and Foreign Policy.* New York: Praeger.

Ambrosius, L. E. 1987. *Woodrow Wilson and the American Diplomatic Tradition: The Treaty Fight in Perspective.* Cambridge: Cambridge University Press.

Americans Talk Security Project (ATS). 1988. *A Series of Surveys of American Voters: Attitudes Concerning National Security Issues.* Washington, D.C.: Daniel Yankelovich Group.

Anderson, P. 1974. *Lineages of the Absolutist State.* London: New Left Books.

Arbatov, A. G. 1993. "Russia's Foreign Policy Alternatives." *International Security* 18:5–43.

Art, R. J. 1991. "A Defensible Defense: America's Grand Strategy After the Cold War." *International Security* 15:5–53.

Ashley, R. K. 1980. *The Political Economy of War and Peace.* London: Frances Pinter.

———. 1984. "The Poverty of Neorealism." *International Organization* 38:225–286.

———. 1989. "Living on the Border Lines: Man, Poststructuralism, and War." In *International/Intertextual Relations: Postmodern Readings of World Politics*, edited by J. Der Derian and M. J. Shapiro, pp. 259–321. Lexington, Mass.: Lexington Books.

Axelrod, R. 1986. "An Evolutionary Approach to Norms." *American Political Science Review* 80:1095–1111.

———, ed. 1976. *The Structure of Decision: The Cognitive Maps of Political Elites.* Princeton, N.J.: Princeton University Press.

Barnett, M. 1990. "High Politics Is Low Politics: The Domestic and Systemic Sources of Israeli Security Policy, 1967–1977." *World Politics* 42:529–562.

Baumol, W., and R. E. Quandt. 1985. "Chaos Models and Their Implications for Forecasting." *Eastern Economic Journal* 11:3–15.

Bennett, A. L. 1991. *International Organizations: Principles and Issues.* 5th ed. Englewood Cliffs, N.J.: Prentice Hall.

Beschloss, M. R., and S. Talbott. 1993. *At the Highest Levels: The Inside Story of the End of the Cold War.* Boston, Mass.: Little, Brown.

Betts, R. K. 1992. "Systems for Peace or Causes of War? Collective Security, Arms Control, and the New Europe." *International Security* 17:5–43.

137

Beyerchen, A. 1988–1989. "Nonlinear Science and the Unfolding of a New Intellectual Voice." *Papers in Comparative Studies* 6:26–29.

———. 1992–1993. "Clausewitz, Nonlinearity, and the End of the Cold War." *International Security* 17:59–90.

Bobbitt, P. 1988. *Democracy and Deterrence: The History and Future of Nuclear Strategy.* New York: St. Martin's.

Bremer, S. A. 1992. "Dangerous Dyads: Conditions Affecting the Likelihood of Interstate War, 1816–1965." *Journal of Conflict Resolution* 36:309–341.

Brodie, B. 1946. *The Absolute Weapon.* New York: Harcourt, Brace.

Bueno de Mesquita, B. 1981. *The War Trap.* New Haven, Conn.: Yale University Press.

Bueno de Mesquita, B., and D. Lalman. 1990. "Domestic Opposition and Foreign War." *American Political Science Review* 84:747–766.

Bunce, V. 1993. "Domestic Reform and International Change: The Gorbachev Reforms in Historical Perspective." *International Organization* 47:107–138.

Burley, A. M. 1993. "Regulating the World: Multilateralism, International Law, and the Projection of the New Deal Regulatory State." In *Multilateralism Matters*, edited by J. G. Ruggie, pp. 125–156. New York: Columbia University Press.

Buzan, B. 1991. *People, States, and Fear: The National Security Problem in International Relations.* 2d ed. Boulder, Colo.: Lynne Rienner.

Calleo, D. P. 1987. *Beyond American Hegemony: The Future of the Western Alliance.* New York: Basic Books.

Cannon, L. 1991. *President Reagan: The Role of a Lifetime.* New York: Simon and Schuster.

Caporaso, J.A. 1993. "International Relations Theory and Multilateralism: The Search for Foundations." In *Multilateralism Matters: The Theory and Praxis of an Institutional Form,* edited by John Gerard Ruggie, pp. 51–90. New York: Columbia University Press.

Carr, E. H. 1939. *The Twenty Years' Crisis, 1919–1939.* London: Macmillan.

Chalmers, M. 1990. "Beyond the Alliance System." *World Policy Journal* 7:215–250.

Christensen, T. J., and J. Snyder. 1990. "Chain Gangs and Passed Bucks: Predicting Alliance Patterns in Multipolarity." *International Organization* 44:137–168.

Claude, Inis L., Jr. 1959. *Swords into Plowshares: The Problems and Progress of International Organization.* 2d rev. ed. New York: Random House.

———. 1962. *Power and International Relations.* New York: Random House.

Cohen, B. C. 1973. *The Public's Impact on Foreign Policy.* Boston, Mass.: Little, Brown.

Cowhey, P. F. 1993a. "Domestic Institutions and the Credibility of International Commitments." *International Organization* 47:299–326.

———. 1993b. "Elect Locally—Order Globally: Domestic Politics and Multilateral Cooperation." In *Multilateralism Matters: The Theory and Praxis of an Institutional Form,* edited by John Gerard Ruggie, pp. 157–200. New York: Columbia University Press.

Cox, R. W. 1987. *Production, Power, and World Order: Social Forces in the Making of History.* New York: Columbia University Press.

Crabb, C. V., Jr. 1986. *Policy-Makers and Critics: Conflicting Theories of American Foreign Policy.* 2d ed. New York: Praeger.

Craig, G. A. 1977. "The United States and the European Balance." In *Two Hundred Years of American Foreign Policy,* edited by W. P. Bundy, pp. 67–89. New York: New York University Press.

Dean, J., and R. W. Forsberg. 1992. "CFE and Beyond: The Future of Conventional Arms Control." *International Security* 17:76–121.

DeConde, A. 1963. *A History of American Foreign Policy.* New York: Scribner's.

Deese, D. A., ed. 1994. *The New Politics of American Foreign Policy.* New York: St. Martin's.

Dehio, L. 1962. *The Precarious Balance: Four Centuries of the European Power Struggle.* New York: Random House.

Deibel, T. L. 1992. "National Strategy and the Continuity of National Interests." In *Grand Strategy and the Decisionmaking Process,* edited by J. C. Gaston, pp. 37–54. Washington, D.C.: National Defense University Press.

DePorte, A. W. 1986. *Europe Between the Superpowers: The Enduring Balance.* New Haven, Conn.: Yale University Press.

Dessler, D. 1989. "What's at Stake in the Agent-Structure Debate?" *International Organization* 43:441–474.

———. 1991. "Beyond Correlations: Toward a Causal Theory of War." *International Studies Quarterly* 35:337–355.

Destler, I. M., L. H. Gelb, and A. Lake. 1984. *Our Own Worst Enemy: The Unmaking of American Foreign Policy.* New York: Simon and Schuster.

de Tocqueville, A. 1969. *Democracy in America,* edited by J. P. Mayer. New York: Doubleday.

Deudney, D., and G. J. Ikenberry. 1991–1992. "The International Sources of Soviet Change." *International Security* 16:74–118.

Deutsch, K. W. 1988. *The Analysis of International Relations.* 3d ed. Englewood Cliffs, N.J.: Prentice Hall.

Diehl, P. F., and G. Goertz. 1988. "Territorial Changes and Militarized Conflict." *Journal of Conflict Resolution* 32:113–122.

Doyle, M. W. 1983. "Kant, Liberal Legacies, and Foreign Affairs." *Philosophy and Public Affairs* 12:205–235.

———. 1986. "Liberalism and World Politics." *American Political Science Review* 80:1151–1169.

Duffy, M., and D. Goodgame. 1992. *Marching in Place: The Status Quo Presidency of George Bush.* New York: Simon and Schuster.

Durch, W. J., ed. 1993. *The Evolution of UN Peacekeeping.* New York: St. Martin's.

Evangelista, M. 1989. "Issue-Area and Foreign Policy Revisited." *International Organization* 43:147–172.

Evans, P. B., H. K. Jacobson, and R. D. Putnam, eds. 1993. *Double-Edged Diplomacy: International Bargaining and Domestic Politics.* Berkeley: University of California Press.

Ferguson, Y. H., and R. W. Mansbach. 1988. *The Elusive Quest: Theory and International Politics.* Columbia: University of South Carolina Press.

Flynn, G., and D. Scheffer. 1990. "Limited Collective Security." *Foreign Policy* 80:77–101.

Foster, G. D. 1992. "A Conceptual Foundation for the Development of Strategy." In *Grand Strategy and the Decisionmaking Process,* edited by J. C. Gaston, pp. 55–76. Washington, D.C.: National Defense University Press.

Friedberg, A. L. 1989. *The Weary Titan: Britain and the Experience of Relative Decline, 1895–1905.* Princeton, N.J.: Princeton University Press.

Gaddis, J. L. 1982. *Strategies of Containment: A Critical Appraisal of Postwar American National Security Policy.* New York: Oxford University Press.

———. 1987. *The Long Peace: Inquiries into the History of the Cold War.* New York: Oxford University Press.

————. 1990. "New Conceptual Approaches to the Study of American Foreign Policy: Interdisciplinary Perspectives." *Diplomatic History* 14:405–423.

————. 1992–1993. "International Relations Theory and the End of the Cold War." *International Security* 17:5–58.

Gartoff, R. L. 1985. *Détente and Confrontation: American-Soviet Relations from Nixon to Reagan.* Washington, D.C.: Brookings.

Gati, C. 1988–1989. "Eastern Europe on Its Own." *Foreign Affairs* 68:99–119.

George, A. L. 1979. "The Causal Nexus Between Cognitive Beliefs and Decision-Making Behavior: The 'Operational Code' Belief System." In *Psychological Models in International Politics*, edited by L. S. Falkowski, pp. 95–124. Boulder, Colo.: Westview Press.

————. 1988a. "Factors Influencing Security Cooperation." In *U.S.–Soviet Security Cooperation*, edited by A. L. George, P. J. Farley, and A. Dallin, pp. 655–678. New York: Oxford University Press.

————. 1988b. "U.S.–Soviet Efforts to Cooperate in Crisis Management and Crisis Avoidance." In *U.S.–Soviet Security Cooperation*, edited by A. L. George, P. J. Farley, and A. Dallin, pp. 581–599. Oxford: Oxford University Press.

————. 1989. "Domestic Constraints on Regime Change in U.S. Foreign Policy: The Need for Policy Legitimacy." In *American Foreign Policy: Theoretical Essays*, edited by G. J. Ikenberry, pp. 583–608. Glenview, Ill.: Scott, Foresman.

————. 1993. *Bridging the Gap: Theory and Practice in Foreign Policy.* Washington, D.C.: United States Institute for Peace.

————, ed. 1983. *Managing U.S–Soviet Rivalry: Problems of Crisis Prevention.* Boulder, Colo.: Westview Press.

————. 1991. *Avoiding War: Problems of Crisis Management.* Boulder, Colo.: Westview Press.

Gerschenkron, A. 1963. *Economic Backwardness in Historical Perspective.* Cambridge, Mass.: Harvard University Press.

Gerth, H. H., and C. W. Mills, eds. 1946. *From Max Weber: Essays in Sociology.* New York: Oxford University Press.

Gilpin, R. 1981. *War and Change in World Politics.* Cambridge: Cambridge University Press.

Goertz, G., and P. F. Diehl. 1993. "Enduring Rivalries: Theoretical Constructs and Empirical Patterns." *International Studies Quarterly* 37:147–172.

Goldgeier, J. M., and M. McFaul. 1992. "A Tale of Two Worlds: Core and Periphery in the Post–Cold War Era." *International Organization* 46:467–492.

Goodby, J. 1991. "A New European Concert: Settling Disputes in CSCE." *Arms Control Today* 21:3–6.

Grieco, J. M., 1988. "Anarchy and the Limits of Cooperation: A Realist Critique of the Newest Liberal Institutionalism." *International Organization* 42:486–507.

Haas, P. M. 1992. "Introduction: Epistemic Communities and International Policy Coordination." *International Organization* 46:1–36.

Harris, O. 1993. "The Collapse of the 'West.'" *Foreign Affairs* 72:41–53.

Hattendorf, J. B. 1991. "Alliance, Encirclement, and Attrition: British Grand Strategy in the War of the Spanish Succession, 1702–1713." In *Grand Strategies in War and* Peace, edited by P. Kennedy, pp. 11–30. New Haven, Conn.: Yale University Press.

Henkin, L. 1972. *Foreign Affairs and the Constitution.* Mineola, N.Y.: Foundation Press.

Herbst, J. 1990. "War and the State in Africa." *International Security* 14:117–139.

Hermann, C. F. 1990. "Changing Course: When Governments Choose to Redirect Foreign Policy." *International Studies Quarterly* 34:3–22.

Herz, J. 1950. "Idealist Internationalism and the Security Dilemma." *World Politics* 2:157–180.

Hinsley, F. H. 1963. *Power and the Pursuit of Peace*. Cambridge: Cambridge University Press.

Hogan, M. J. 1984. "Revival and Reform: America's Twentieth-Century Search for a New Economic Order Abroad." *Diplomatic History* 8:287–310.

———. 1987. *The Marshall Plan: America, Britain, and the Reconstruction of Western Europe, 1947–1952*. Cambridge: Cambridge University Press.

Holsti, K. J. 1991. *Peace and War: Armed Conflicts and International Order, 1648–1989*. Cambridge: Cambridge University Press.

Hopf, T. 1991. "Polarity, the Offense-Defense Balance and War." *American Political Science Review* 85:475–494.

Howard, M. 1991. "British Grand Strategy in World War I." In *Grand Strategies in War and Peace*, edited by P. Kennedy, pp. 31–42. New Haven, Conn.: Yale University Press.

Huntington, S. P. 1961. *The Common Defense: Strategic Programs in National Politics*. New York: Columbia University Press.

———. 1987–1988. "Coping with the Lippmann Gap." *Foreign Affairs* 66:453–477.

———. 1991. *The Third Wave: Democratization in the Late Twentieth Century*. Norman: University of Oklahoma Press.

Hyland, W. G. 1992. "Foreign Affairs at Seventy." *Foreign Affairs* 71:171–193.

Ikenberry, G. J. 1989. *American Foreign Policy: Theoretical Essays*. Glenview, Ill.: Scott, Foresman.

Ikenberry, G. J., and C. A. Kupchan. 1990. "Socialization and Hegemonic Power." *International Organization* 44:283–316.

Ikenberry, G. J., D. A. Lake, and M. Mastanduno, eds. 1988. *The State and American Foreign Economic Policy*. Ithaca, N.Y.: Cornell University Press.

International Institute for Strategic Studies (IISS). 1992. *The Military Balance, 1992–1993*. London: Brassey's.

Jackson, R. H. 1990. *Quasi-States: Sovereignty, International Relations, and the Third World*. Cambridge: Cambridge University Press.

Jentleson, B. W. 1992. "The Pretty Prudent Public: Post Post-Vietnam American Opinion on the Use of Military Force." *International Studies Quarterly* 36:49–74.

Jervis, R. 1978. "Cooperation Under the Security Dilemma." *World Politics* 30:167–214.

———. 1983. "Security Regimes." In *International Regimes*, edited by S. D. Krasner, pp. 173–194. Ithaca, N.Y.: Cornell University Press.

———. 1985. "From Balance to Concert: A Study of International Security Cooperation." *World Politics* 28:58–79.

———. 1988. "Realism, Game Theory, and Cooperation." *World Politics* 40:317–349.

———. 1989. *The Meaning of the Nuclear Revolution*. Ithaca, N.Y.: Cornell University Press.

———. 1991–1992. "The Future of World Politics: Will It Resemble the Past?" *International Security* 16:39–73.

Jervis, R., and J. Snyder, eds. 1991. *Dominoes and Bandwagons: Strategic Beliefs and Great Power Competition in the Eurasian Rimland*. New York: Oxford University Press.

Kahler, M. 1992. "Multilateralism with Small and Large Numbers." *International Organization* 46:681–708.

Kanet, R. E. 1990. "Superpower Cooperation in Eastern Europe." Presented at the annual meeting of the International Studies Association, Washington, D.C., April 11–15.

Katzenstein, P. J. 1977. "Conclusion: Domestic Structures and Strategies of Foreign Economic Policy." *International Organization* 31:879–920.

Katzenstein, P. J., and N. Okawara. 1993. "Japan's National Security: Structures, Norms, and Policies." *International Security* 17:84–118.

Kaysen, C. 1990. "Is War Obsolete? A Review Essay." *International Security* 14: 42–64.

Kegley, C. W., Jr. 1987. "Decision Regimes and the Comparative Study of Foreign Policy." In *New Directions in the Study of Foreign Policy*, edited by C. F. Hermann, C. W. Kegley, Jr., and J. N. Rosenau, pp. 247–268. Boston, Mass.: Allen and Unwin.

Kegley, C. W., Jr., and G. Raymond. 1993. *A Multipolar Peace?* New York: St. Martin's.

Kegley, C. W., Jr., and E. R. Wittkopf. 1991. *American Foreign Policy: Pattern and Process*. 4th ed. New York: St. Martin's.

Kennan, G. F. 1951. *American Diplomacy, 1900–1950*. New York: New American Library.

Kennedy, P. 1987. *The Rise and Fall of the Great Powers*. New York: Random House.

———, ed. 1991. *Grand Strategies in Peace and War*. New Haven, Conn.: Yale University Press.

Keohane, R. O. 1984. *After Hegemony: Cooperation and Discord in the World Political Economy*. Princeton, N.J.: Princeton University Press.

———. 1986. "Theory of World Politics: Structural Realism and Beyond." In *Neorealism and Its Critics*, edited by R. O. Keohane, pp. 158–203. New York: Columbia University Press.

———. 1989. *International Institutions and State Power*. Boulder, Colo.: Westview Press.

Keohane, R. O., and J. S. Nye. 1989. *Power and Interdependence*. 2d ed. Boston, Mass.: Little, Brown.

Key, V. O. 1961. *Public Opinion and American Democracy*. New York: Knopf.

Kissinger, H. A. 1956. "Reflections on American Diplomacy." *Foreign Affairs* 35: 37–56.

Klein, R. A. 1974. *Sovereign Equality Among States: The History of an Idea*. Toronto: University of Toronto Press.

Krasner, S. D. 1978. *Defending the National Interest: Raw Materials, Investments, and U.S. Foreign Policy*. Princeton, N.J.: Princeton University Press.

———. 1991. "Global Communications and National Power: Life on the Pareto Frontier." *World Politics* 43:336–366.

———, ed. 1983. *International Regimes*. Ithaca, N.Y.: Cornell University Press.

Kratochwil, F. 1993. "Norms Versus Numbers: Multilateralism and the Rationalist and Reflexivist Approaches to Institutions—A Unilateral Plea for Communicative Rationality." In *Multilateralism Matters*, edited by J. G. Ruggie, pp. 443–474. New York: Columbia University Press.

Krauthammer, C. 1990–1991. "The Unipolar Moment." *Foreign Affairs* 70:23–33.

Kupchan, C. A., and C. A. Kupchan. 1991. "Concerts, Collective Security, and the Future of Europe." *International Security* 16:114–161.

Lamb, C. J. 1988. *How to Think About Arms Control, Disarmament, and Defense*. Englewood Cliffs, N.J.: Prentice Hall.

Larson, D. W. 1985. *Origins of Containment: A Psychological Explanation*. Princeton, N.J.: Princeton University Press.

Lebow, R. N., and J. G. Stein. 1989. "Rational Deterrence Theory: I Think, Therefore I Deter." *World Politics* 41:208–224.

Leffler, M. P. 1979. *The Elusive Quest: America's Pursuit of European Stability and French Security, 1919–1933.* Chapel Hill: University of North Carolina.

Leigh, M. 1976. *Mobilizing Consent: Public Opinion and American Foreign Policy.* Westport, Conn.: Greenwood.

Levin, N. G., Jr. 1968. *Woodrow Wilson and World Politics.* New York: Oxford University Press.

Levy, J. S. 1983. *War in the Modern Great Power System, 1495–1975.* Lexington: University Press of Kentucky.

———. 1989. "The Causes of War: A Review of Theories and Evidence." In *Behavior, Society, and Nuclear War,* vol. 1, edited by P. E. Tetlock, J. L. Husbands, R. Jervis, P. C. Stern, and C. Tilly, pp. 209–333. New York: Oxford University Press.

Lippmann, W. 1943. *U.S. Foreign Policy: Shield of the Republic.* Boston, Mass.: Little, Brown.

Lipson, C. 1984. "International Cooperation in Economics and Security Affairs." *World Politics* 37:1–23.

Luard, E. 1986. *War in International Society.* New Haven, Conn.: Yale University Press.

Maier, C. S. 1981. "The Two Postwar Eras and the Conditions for Stability in Twentieth-Century Western Europe." *American Historical Review* 86:327–352.

Mandelbaum, M. 1989. "Ending the Cold War." *Foreign Affairs* 68:16–36.

Maoz, Z., and N. Abdolali. 1989. "Regime Types and International Conflict, 1816–1976." *Journal of Conflict Resolution* 33:3–35.

Maoz, Z., and B. Russett. 1993. "Normative and Structural Causes of Democratic Peace, 1946–1986." *American Political Science Review* 87:624–638.

Maresca, J. J. 1985. *To Helsinki: The Conference on Security and Cooperation in Europe, 1973–75.* Durham, N.C.: Duke University Press.

———. 1988. "Helsinki Accord, 1975." In *U.S.–Soviet Security Cooperation,* edited by A. L. George, P. J. Farley, and A. Dallin, pp. 106–122. New York: Oxford University Press.

Martin, L. L. 1992. *Coercive Cooperation: Explaining Multilateral Economic Sanctions.* Princeton, N.J.: Princeton University Press.

———. 1993. "The Rational State Choice of Multilateralism." In *Multilateralism Matters,* edited by J. G. Ruggie, pp. 91–121. New York: Columbia University Press.

Mastanduno, M., D. A. Lake, and G. J. Ikenberry. 1989. "Toward a Realist Theory of State Action." *International Studies Quarterly* 33:457–474.

McCormick, J. M. 1985. *American Foreign Policy and American Values.* Itasca, Ill: Peacock.

McCormick, T. J. 1989. *America's Half-Century: United States Foreign Policy in the Cold War.* Baltimore, Md.: Johns Hopkins University Press.

Mearsheimer, J. J. 1990. "Back to the Future: Instability in Europe after the Cold War." *International Security* 15:5–56.

Miller, B. 1992. "Explaining Great Power Cooperation in Conflict Management." *World Politics* 45:1–46.

Milner, H. 1992. "International Theories of Cooperation Among Nations: Strengths and Weaknesses." *World Politics* 44:466–496.

Modelski, G. 1978. "The Long Cycle of Global Politics and the Nation-State." *Comparative Studies in Society and History* 20:214–235.

Modelski, G., and P. M. Morgan. 1985. "Understanding Global War." *Journal of Conflict Resolution* 29:391–417.

Monroe, J. 1823/1896. "Address to the Congress, December 2, 1823." In *A Compilation of the Messages and Papers of the Presidents, 1789–1897*, edited by J. D. Richardson, pp. 207–220. Washington, D.C.: Government Printing Office, 1896.

Moore, B., Jr. 1966. *Social Origins of Dictatorship and Democracy*. Boston, Mass.: Little, Brown.

Morgan, P. M. 1993. "Multilateralism and Security Prospects in Europe." In *Multilateralism Matters*, edited by J. G. Ruggie, pp. 327–364. New York: Columbia University Press.

Morgenthau, H. 1951/1989. "The Mainsprings of American Foreign Policy." In *American Foreign Policy: Theoretical Essays*, edited by G. J. Ikenberry, pp. 634–643. Glenview, Ill.: Scott, Foresman.

Morgenthau, H., and K. Thompson. 1985. *Politics Among Nations*. 6th ed. New York: Knopf.

Most, B. A., and H. Starr. 1980. "Diffusion, Reinforcement, Geo-politics, and the Spread of War." *American Political Science Review* 74:932–946.

―――. 1989. *Inquiry, Logic, and International Politics*. New York: Columbia University Press.

Mueller, H. 1991. "A United Nations of Europe and North America." *Arms Control Today* 21:3–8.

Mueller, J. 1989a. "A New Concert of Europe." *Foreign Policy* 77:3–16.

―――. 1989b. *Retreat from Doomsday*. New York: Basic Books.

Nixon, R. M. 1988–1989. "American Foreign Policy: The Bush Agenda." *Foreign Affairs* 68:199–219.

Nye, J. S., Jr. 1987. "Nuclear Learning and U.S.–Soviet Security Regimes." *International Organization* 41:371–402.

―――. 1990. *Bound to Lead: The Changing Nature of American Power*. New York: Basic Books.

Olson, M. 1965. *The Logic of Collective Action*. Cambridge, Mass.: Harvard University Press.

Osgood, R. E. 1953. *Ideals and Self-Interest in America's Foreign Relations*. Chicago, Ill.: Chicago University Press.

Osgood, R. E., and R. W. Tucker. 1967. *Force, Order, and Justice*. Baltimore, Md.: Johns Hopkins University Press.

Oye, K. A. 1985. "Explaining Cooperation Under Anarchy: Hypotheses and Strategies." *World Politics* 38:1–24.

Paine, T. 1775/1938. "Common Sense." In *Writings of Thomas Paine*, edited by C. Van Doren, pp. 1–40. New York: Carlton House.

Paterson, T. G., J. G. Clifford, and K. J. Hagan. 1991. *American Foreign Policy: A History Since 1900*. 3d rev. ed. Lexington, Mass.: D. C. Heath.

Perrow, C. 1984. *Normal Accidents*. New York: Basic Books.

Pfaff, W. 1993. "Invitation to War." *Foreign Affairs* 72:97–109.

Posen, B. R. 1984. *The Sources of Military Doctrine: France, Britain, and Germany Between the World Wars*. Ithaca, N.Y.: Cornell University Press.

―――. 1993. "The Security Dilemma and Ethnic Conflict." *Survival* 35:27–47.

Puchala, D. J. 1990. "Woe to the Orphans of the Scientific Revolution." *Journal of International Affairs* 44:59–80.

Putnam, R. D. 1988. "Diplomacy and Domestic Politics: The Logic of Two-Level Games." *International Organization* 42:427–460.

Ramet, S. P. 1992. "War in the Balkans." *Foreign Affairs* 71:79–98.

Rapkin, D. P. 1987. "World Leadership." In *Exploring Long Cycles*, edited by G. Modelski, pp. 129–157. Boulder, Colo.: Lynne Rienner.

Ray, J. L. 1989. "The Abolition of Slavery and the End of International War." *International Organization* 43:405–440.

Risse-Kappen, T. 1991. "Public Opinion, Domestic Structure, and Foreign Policy in Liberal Democracies." *World Politics* 43:479–512.

———. 1993. "Masses and Leaders: Public Opinion, Domestic Structures, and Foreign Policy." In *The New Politics of American Foreign Policy*, edited by D. A. Deese, pp. 238–261. New York: St. Martin's.

Rosati, J. L. 1987. *The Carter Administration's Quest for Global Community*. Columbia: University of South Carolina Press.

Rosecrance, R. N. 1986. *The Rise of the Trading State*. New York: Basic Books.

———. 1992. "A New Concert of Powers." *Foreign Affairs* 71(2): 64–82.

Rosenau, J. N. 1984. "Before Cooperation: Hegemons, Regimes, and Habit-Driven Actors in World Politics." *International Organization* 40:849–894.

———. 1990. *Turbulence in World Politics*. Princeton, N.J.: Princeton University Press.

Rostow, E. V. 1993. *Toward Managed Peace: The National Security of the United States, 1759 to Present*. New Haven, Conn.: Yale University Press.

Ruggie, J. G. 1983. "International Regimes, Transactions, and Change: Embedded Liberalism in the Postwar Economic Order." In *International Regimes*, edited by S. D. Krasner, pp. 195–232. Ithaca, N.Y.: Cornell University Press.

———. 1992. "Multilateralism: The Anatomy of an Institution." *International Organization* 46:561–598.

———. 1993. *Multilateralism Matters: The Theory and Praxis of an Institutional Form*. New York: Columbia University Press.

Rummel, R. J. 1983. "Libertarianism and International Violence." *Journal of Conflict Resolution* 27:27–71.

Russett, B. 1993. *Grasping the Democratic Peace: Principles for a Post–Cold War World*. Princeton, N.J.: Princeton University Press.

Schlesinger, A. M., Jr. 1986. *The Cycles of American History*. Boston, Mass.: Houghton Mifflin.

Schneider, W. 1992. "The Old Politics and the New World Order." In *Eagle in a New World: American Grand Strategy in the Post–Cold War Era*, edited by K. A. Oye, R. J. Lieber, and D. Rothchild, pp. 35–68. New York: HarperCollins.

Schultz, G. P. 1993. *Turmoil and Triumph: My Years as Secretary of State*. New York: Scribner's.

Singer, J. D., Stuart A. Bremer, and John Stuckey. 1972. "Capability Distribution, Uncertainty, and Major Power War, 1820–1965." In *Peace, War, and Numbers*, edited by B. Russett, pp. 19–48. Beverly Hills, Calif.: Sage.

Siverson, R., and J. King 1979. "Alliances and the Expansion of War." In *To Augur Well: Early Warning Indicators in World Politics*, edited by J. D. Singer and M. D. Wallace, pp. 37–49. Beverly Hills, Calif.: Sage.

Small, M., and J. D. Singer. 1976. "The War Proneness of Democratic Regimes." *Jerusalem Journal of International Relations* 1:41–64.

———. 1982. *Resort to Arms: International and Civil Wars, 1816–1980*. Beverly Hills, Calif.: Sage.

Snidal, D. 1985. "The Limits of Hegemonic Stability Theory." *International Organization* 39:579–614.

Snyder, G. H. 1984. "The Security Dilemma in Alliance Politics." *World Politics* 36:461–495.

Snyder, J. 1989. "International Leverage on Soviet Domestic Change." *World Politics* 42:1–30.

————. 1990. "Averting Anarchy in the New Europe." *International Security* 14:5–41.

————. 1991. *Myths of Empire*. Ithaca, N.Y.: Cornell University Press.

————. 1993. "Nationalism and the Crisis of the Post-Soviet State." *Survival* 35:5–26.

Snyder, J., and R. Jervis, eds. 1992. *Coping with Complexity in the International System*. Boulder, Colo.: Westview Press.

Spiezio, K. E. 1992. "Long Major Power Peace: The Need for a Comparative Perspective." Paper delivered at the annual meeting of the Peace Science Society (International) Pittsburgh, Penn., November, 1992.

Starr, H., and B. Most. 1983. "Contagion and Border Effects on Contemporary African Conflict." *Comparative Political Studies* 16:92–117.

Stein, A. A. 1983. "Coordination and Collaboration: Regimes in an Anarchic World." In *International Regimes*, edited by S. D. Krasner, pp. 115–140. Ithaca, N.Y.: Cornell University Press.

Stein, J. G. 1985. "Detection and Defection: Security Regimes and the Management of International Conflict." *International Journal* 60:607–624.

————. 1991. "Deterrence and Reassurance." In *Behavior, Society, and Nuclear War*, vol. 2, edited by P. E. Tetlock, J. L. Husbands, R. Jervis, P. C. Stern, and C. Tilly, pp. 8–72. New York: Oxford University Press.

Steinberg, J. B. 1993. "Yugoslavia." In *Collective Restraint: Collective Intervention in Internal Conflicts*, edited by L. F. Damrosch, pp. 27–76. New York: Council on Foreign Relations Press.

Stockholm International Peace Research Institute. 1992. *World Armaments and Disarmament*. London: Taylor and Francis.

Thompson, K. 1953. "Collective Security Re-examined." *American Political Science Review* 47:753–772.

Tilly, C., ed. 1975. *The Formation of National States in Western Europe*. Princeton, N.J.: Princeton University Press.

Tucker, R. W. 1972. *A New Isolationism: Threat or Promise?* Washington, D.C.: Potomac Associates.

————. 1988–1989. "Reagan's Foreign Policy." *Foreign Affairs* 68:1–27.

Tucker, R. W., and D. C. Hendrickson. 1992. *The Imperial Temptation: The New World Order and America's Purpose*. New York: Council on Foreign Relations Press.

Ullman, R. 1991. *Securing Europe*. Princeton, N.J.: Princeton University Press.

Van Evera, S. 1990–1991. "Primed for Peace: Europe After the Cold War." *International Security* 15:7–57.

Vasquez, J. A. 1986. *Evaluating U.S. Foreign Policy*. New York: Praeger.

Wallerstein, I. 1974. "The Rise and Future Demise of the World Capitalist System: Concepts for Comparative Analysis." *Comparative Studies in Society and History* 16:387–415.

Walt, S.M. 1987. *The Origins of Alliances*. Ithaca, N.Y.: Cornell University Press.

————. 1989. "The Case for Finite Containment: Analyzing U.S. Grand Strategy." *International Security* 14:5–49.

Waltz, K. N. 1967. *Foreign Policy and Democratic Politics*. Boston, Mass.: Little, Brown.

————. 1979. *Theory of International Politics*. Reading, Mass.: Addison-Wesley.

————. 1983. "Toward Nuclear Peace." In *The Use of Force*, edited by R. J. Art and K. N. Waltz, pp. 573–601. Lanham, Md.: University Press of America.

————. 1990. "Nuclear Myths and Political Realities." *American Political Science Review* 84:731–746.

————. 1993. "The Emerging Structure of International Politics." *International Security* 18:44–79.

Washington, G. 1796/1940. "The Farewell Address." In *The Writings of George Washington from the Original Manuscript Sources, 1745–1799*, edited by J. C. Fitzpatrick, pp. 214–238. Washington, D.C.: Government Printing Office, 1940.

Weber, S. 1992. "Shaping the Postwar Balance of Power: Multilateralism in NATO." *International Organization* 46:633–680.

Weisband, E. 1973. *The Ideology of American Foreign Policy: A Paradigm of Lockian Liberalism*. Beverly Hills, Calif.: Sage.

Wendt, A. 1992. "Anarchy Is What States Make of It: The Social Construction of Power Politics." *International Organization* 46:391–426.

Williams, W. A. 1962. *The Tragedy of American Diplomacy*. New York: Norton.

Wittkopf, E. R. 1990. *Faces of Internationalism: Public Opinion and American Foreign Policy*. Durham, N.C.: Duke University Press.

Wolfers, A. 1962. *Discord and Collaboration: Essays on International Politics*. Baltimore, Md.: Johns Hopkins University Press.

Yankelovich, D. 1992. "Foreign Policy After the Election." *Foreign Affairs* 71: 1–12.

Yergin, A. 1977. *Shattered Peace: The Origins of the Cold War and the National Security State*. Boston, Mass.: Houghton Mifflin.

Young, O. R. 1989. *International Cooperation: Building Regimes for Natural Resources and the Environment*. Ithaca, N.Y.: Cornell University Press.

————. 1991. "Political Leadership and Regime Formation: On the Development of Institutions in International Society." *International Organization* 45:281–308.

Zelikow, P. 1992. "The New Concert of Europe." *Survival* 34:12–30.

Newspaper Articles

Devroy, A. 1994. "Pact Reached to Dismantle Ukraine's Nuclear Force." *Washington Post* (January 11): p. A1.

Dewar, H. 1993a. "Senate Vote on Pullout Delayed." *Washington Post* (October 7): p. A39.

————. 1993b. "Senators Approve Troop Compromise." *Washington Post* (October 21): p. A1.

Drozdiak, W. 1993. "NATO Balks at Opening Pact to E. Europe." *Washington Post* (September 1): p. A25.

————. 1994. "European Nations Awaiting Sign of Renewed Commitment from U.S." *Washington Post* (January 9): pp. A31–32.

Drozdiak, W., and D. Williams. 1994. "NATO Offers Partnership to East European Nations." *Washington Post* (January 11): p. A1.

Gellman, B. 1993a. "Wider U.N. Police Role Supported." *Washington Post* (August 5): p. A1.

————. 1993b. "U.S. Is Reconsidering Putting Combat Troops Under U.N. Command." *Washington Post* (September 22): p. A32.

Hiatt, F. 1992. "Six Ex-Soviet States Sign Collective Security Pact." *Washington Post* (May 16): p. A16.

————. 1994. "A-Arms in Ukraine Decaying, Russians Say." *Washington Post* (January 19): p. A21.

Lippman, T. W. 1993. "Christopher Talks 'Partnership' in East." *Washington Post* (October 22): p. A28.

Marcus, R., and H. Dewar. 1993. "Clinton Tells Congress to Back Off." *Washington Post* (October 19): p. A1.

Preston, J. 1993a. "Violations Soaring in 'No-Fly Zone.'" *Washington Post* (January 14): p. A16.

———. 1993b. "U.N. Officials Scale Back Peacemaking Ambitions." *Washington Post* (October 28): p. A39.

Samuelson, R. J. 1994. "Clinton—Passionate Hypocrite." *Washington Post* (January 19): p. A19.

Shapiro, M. 1993. "Ukraine Nominally Ratifies START I." *Washington Post* (November 19): p. A45.

Smith, R. J. 1993. "U.S. Will Seek to Mediate Ex-Soviet States' Disputes." *Washington Post* (August 5): p. A1.

Williams, D. 1993a. "Russia Vows Bosnia Peace Role: Sidesteps U.S. Military Force Proposal." *Washington Post* (May 6): p. A40.

———. 1993b. "Russia Asserts Role in Ex-Soviet Republics." *Washington Post* (October 29): p. A25.

———. 1994. "Clinton Will Seek Allies' Support for 'Evolutionary' NATO Expansion." *Washington Post* (January 9): pp. A31–32.

Williams, D., and J. M. Goshko. 1993. "Reduced U.S. World Role Outlined but Soon Altered." *Washington Post* (May 26): p. A1.

Williams, D., and L. Hockstader. 1994. "NATO Seeks to Reassure East as Russia Warns Against Expansion." *Washington Post* (January 6): p. A16.

Speeches and Public Statements

Albright, M. 1993a. "Cooperative Security and the United Nations." Speech to the Council on Foreign Relations, June 11, 1993. *Foreign Policy Bulletin* (September/October) 4:33–35.

———. 1993b. "The Need for U.N. Reform." Speech to the Foreign Policy Association, June 8, 1993. *Foreign Policy Bulletin* (September/October) 4:30–33.

———. 1993c. "Statement to the Subcommittees on Europe and the Middle East and on International Security, International Organizations, and Human Rights." U.S. House of Representatives, May 3, 1993. *Foreign Policy Bulletin* (July/August) 4:65–67.

Aspin, L. 1993. "Remarks by Honorable Les Aspin, Secretary of Defense, to the Atlantic Council of the United States, December 3, 1993." U.S. Department of Defense Information Office.

Baker, J. A. 1991a. "America and the Collapse of the Soviet Empire: What Has to Be Done." Speech at Princeton University, December 12, 1991. *Foreign Policy Bulletin* (January/April 1992) 2:17–23.

———. 1991b. "The Euro-Atlantic Architecture: From West to East." Address at the Aspen Institute, Berlin, June 18, 1991. *Foreign Policy Bulletin* (July/August) 2:61–65.

———. 1992a. "Press Conference at Helsinki Summit, July 9, 1992." *Foreign Policy Bulletin* (September/October) 3:63.

———. 1992b. "Start Protocol Signed by Byelarus, Kazakhstan, Russia, Ukraine, and U.S. at Lisbon, May 23, 1992." Statement to the press, May 23, 1992. *Foreign Policy Bulletin* (July/August) 3:54.

Bush, G. 1991a. "Address at Maxwell Air Force Base, War College, Montgomery, AL, April 13, 1991." *Foreign Policy Bulletin* (May/June) 1:32–34.

————. 1991b. "United Nations: The Challenge of the 'Resumption of History.'" Address to the UN General Assembly, September 23, 1991. *Foreign Policy Bulletin* (September/October) 2:71–73.

————. 1992a. "Joint News Conference [with Boris Yeltsin], June 17, 1992." *Foreign Policy Bulletin* (July/August) 3:18–23.

————. 1992b. "The United Nations: Forging a Genuine Global Community." Address to the General Assembly, September 21, 1992. *Foreign Policy Bulletin* (November/December) 3:59–62.

Byrd, R. "Senate Debates U.S. Role in Somalia, September 8, 1993." *Foreign Policy Bulletin* (November/December) 4:19–21.

Christopher, W. 1993a. "Address to the North Atlantic Cooperation Council, Athens, June 11, 1993." *Foreign Policy Bulletin*, (September/October) 4:54–55.

————. 1993b. "Intervention at a Special Meeting of the North Atlantic Council, Brussels, February 26, 1993." *Foreign Policy Bulletin* (May/June) 3:54–56.

————. 1993c. "Intervention at NATO's Foreign Ministers Meeting, Athens, June 8, 1993." *Foreign Policy Bulletin* (September/October) 4:20–23.

————. 1993d. "Press Conference, February 10, 1993." *Foreign Policy Bulletin* (January/April) 3:76–79.

————. 1993e. "Testimony During the Senate Foreign Relations Committee Confirmation Hearings, January 13, 1993." *Foreign Policy Bulletin* (January/April) 3:6–13.

————. 1993f. "U.S. Leadership and Support of Russia." Speech at the Hubert H. Humphrey Institute of Public Affairs, University of Minnesota, May 27, 1993. *Foreign Policy Bulletin* (July/August) 4:45–47.

————. 1994. "NATO Plus." *Washington Post* (January 9): p. C7.

Clinton, B. 1991. "A New Covenant for American Security, Georgetown University, December 12, 1991." *Foreign Policy Bulletin* (November/December) 3:2–8.

————. 1992a. "Foreign Policy Association Speech, April 1, 1992." *Foreign Policy Bulletin* (November/December) 3:8–12.

————. 1992b. "Los Angeles World Affairs Council Speech, August 13, 1992." *Foreign Policy Bulletin* (November/December) 3:12–17.

————. 1993a. "President Clinton's Television Address, October 7, 1993." *Foreign Policy Bulletin* (November/December) 4:32–34.

————. 1993b. "President-Elect Clinton's Remarks to the Diplomatic Corps, January 18, 1993." *Foreign Policy Bulletin* (January/April) 3:4–6.

————. 1993c. "President's Address to U.N. General Assembly, September 27, 1993." *Foreign Policy Bulletin* (November/December) 4:49–53.

————. 1993d. "President's Speech to American Society of Newspaper Editors, April 1, 1993." *Foreign Policy Bulletin* (May/June) 3:21–24.

————. 1994. "A New Security—Built on Integration." *Washington Post* (January 10): p. A11.

Eagleburger, L. 1992. "Address Before North Atlantic Council Ministerial Meeting, Brussels, December 18, 1992." *Foreign Policy Bulletin* (January/April 1993) 3:116.

Fitzwater, M. 1992a. "Open Skies, March 24, 1992." *Foreign Policy Bulletin* (May/June) 2:38–39.

————. 1992b. "White House Statement on CFE-1A Agreement." *Foreign Policy Bulletin* (September/October) 3:44–45.

Kozyrev, A. 1993. "And Now: Partnership with Russia's Democrats." *Washington Post* (October 10): p. C7.

Lake, A. 1993. "National Security Advisor Lake at Johns Hopkins School of Advanced International Studies, September 21, 1993." *Foreign Policy Bulletin* (November/December) 4:39–46.

U.S. Department of State. 1989. *American Foreign Policy: Current Documents (AFP)*. Washington, D.C.: Government Printing Office.

———. 1990. *American Foreign Policy: Current Documents*. Washington D.C.: Government Printing Office.

Treaties and International Commitments

"Camp David Declaration, February 1, 1992." *Foreign Policy Bulletin* (January/April) 2:48–49.

"Charter for American-Russian Partnership and Friendship, June 17, 1992." *Foreign Policy Bulletin* (July/August 1993) 3:12–14.

Conference on Security and Cooperation in Europe (CSCE). November 17, 1990. "Concluding Document of the Vienna Negotiations on CBSMs." *American Foreign Policy: Current Documents.* Washington, D.C.: Government Printing Office, pp. 289–292.

———. November 21, 1990. "Charter of Paris for a New Europe." *Foreign Policy Bulletin* (January/April 1991) 1:75–80.

———. January 30, 1992. "Prague Document." *Foreign Policy Bulletin* (January/April) 2:74–76.

———. July 10, 1992. "Helsinki Summit Declaration." *Foreign Policy Bulletin* (September/October) 3:58–61.

"Joint Announcement of Five-Nation Action Program, May 22, 1993." *Foreign Policy Bulletin* (July/August) 4:13–16.

"Joint Understanding on Reductions in Strategic Offensive Arms." *Foreign Policy Bulletin* (July/August 1992) 3:14–15.

North Atlantic Council. July 6, 1990. "London Declaration." *American Foreign Policy: Current Documents*. Washington, D.C.: Government Printing Office, pp. 275–278.

———. November 8, 1991. "Rome Declaration." *Foreign Policy Bulletin* (January/April 1992) 2:55–58.

———. June 4, 1992. "Oslo Communique." *Foreign Policy Bulletin* (July/August) 3:61–63.

"Treaty on Conventional Armed Forces in Europe, November 19, 1990." *Arms Control Today* (1991): 21.

"Treaty on the Final Settlement with Respect to Germany, September 12, 1990." *Foreign Policy Bulletin* (November/December) 3:1–4.

"Vancouver Declaration, April 4, 1993." *Foreign Policy Bulletin* (May/June) 3:27–28.

INDEX